Creating E-Learning Games with Unity

Develop your own 3D e-learning game using gamification, systems design, and gameplay programming techniques

David Horachek

[PACKT] open source *
PUBLISHING
community experience distilled

BIRMINGHAM - MUMBAI

Creating E-Learning Games with Unity

First published: March 2014

Production Reference: 1180314

Published by Packt Publishing Ltd.
Livery Place
35 Livery Street
Birmingham B3 2PB, UK.

ISBN 978-1-84969-342-4

www.packtpub.com

Cover Image by Parag Kadam (paragvkadam@gmail.com)

Credits

Author
David Horachek

Reviewers
Neeraj Jadhav
Alankar Pradhan
K. Aava Rani
Ranpariya Ankur J. [PAHeartBeat]

Acquisition Editor
Joanne Fitzpatrick

Content Development Editor
Chalini Snega Victor

Technical Editors
Arwa Manasawala
Manal Pednekar
Anand Singh
Ankita Thakur

Copy Editors
Sarang Chari
Brandt D'Mello
Mradula Hegde

Project Coordinator
Binny K. Babu

Proofreader
Simran Bhogal

Indexer
Hemangini Bari

Graphics
Ronak Dhruv
Yuvraj Mannari
Abhinash Sahu

Production Coordinator
Shantanu Zagade

Cover Work
Shantanu Zagade

About the Author

David Horachek is a video game software developer with over 13 years of experience in programming arcade, home console, and portable games. He has programmed game projects published by Midway Games, EA, Ubisoft, SEGA, and others. He develops games under the Arbelos Interactive label.

I would like to thank my wife Allison and my family for their encouragement and support, the team at Packt Publishing for their patience and advice, and aspiring e-learning game programmers for their work to come.

About the Reviewers

Neeraj Jadhav did his Bachelors in Computer Engineering from Mumbai University and Masters in Computer Science from University of Houston-Clear Lake. He has been working as a software developer for three years. His interests primarily lie in software development with Java and C# as well as web development with HTML 5, CSS 3, jQuery, and JavaScript. During his graduate years, he worked on developing games using Unity's 3D game engine with JavaScript and C#.

Alankar Pradhan is from Mumbai, Maharashtra, and went to Indian Education Society's CPV High School. He is an ambitious person who loves interacting with new people, travelling, spending leisure time with friends, or playing games on both his PC and mobile. Games have been always a passion in his life. More than just playing the game, his main curiosity is how things work. Hence, he decided to pursue his career in the same field. He graduated with BSc Honors in Software Development from Sheffield Hallam University, UK. He is currently pursuing an advanced course in game programming (BAC+5 Equivalent) from DSK Supinfogame, where he is undertaking industry-oriented projects to enhance his skill set and giving his best in doing so. He worked as a game programming intern at The Walt Disney Company India Pvt Ltd. During his internship, he worked on a live project, called Hitout Heroes, where he was responsible for integration of small gameplay modules and then social integration of Facebook into the game, but later on, the whole UI implementation, working, flow, and mechanism was managed solely by him. At the end, he was responsible for bug solving and memory management. His name was added in the credits due to his accomplishments.

He has worked in many small projects in team as well as individually, thus sharpening his own skills in various languages, such as C#, C++, Java, Unreal Script, Python, Lua, Groovy/Grails, and HTML5/CSS. He is familiar with engines such as Unity3D, Unreal Development Kit, and Visual Studio and also SDKs such as NetBeans, Eclipse, and Wintermute. Recently, in 2013, his dissertation on *Comparison between Python and Lua in Gaming Industry* got published as a book.

More to this, he even likes to read, listen to music, and write poems and rap songs at times. He has his own website at `http://alan.poetrycraze.com` where he posts his poems and has also published a book called *The Art Of Lost Words*, which is available on Amazon.com.

> We are so often caught up with our goals that we forget to appreciate the journey, especially the people we meet on the way. Appreciation is a wonderful feeling; it's way better if we don't overlook it. I hereby take this opportunity to acknowledge the people who directed me and inspired me in this initiative. I would like to express hearty thanks to my parents, who instilled and believed in me always. I am also thankful to my friends for their constant support and encouraging words that helped me to reach this level. Last but not least, I would like to thank all the people who are directly or indirectly involved in this and helped me in one or the other way.

K. Aava Rani is a co-founder of CulpzLab Pvt Ltd., a software company having 10 years of experience in game technologies. A successful blogger and technologist, she switched her focus to game development in 2004. Since then, she has produced a number of game titles and has provided art and programming solutions to Unity developers across the globe. She is based in New Delhi, India. She has been a recipient of several prestigious awards including Adobe for game technology expert 2012 and SmartFoxServer for her articles. She has experience in various technologies.

Aava is the co-founder of CulpzLab, a software development company of highly skilled professionals in web, game development, and interactive media. Founded in 2010, CulpzLab has proven itself to be a reliable technology partner for its clients. Currently, CulpzLab employs over 50 people and is based in New Delhi, India.

CulpzLab is a leading, custom (bespoke) process-driven software solutions provider that has helped and partnered with many reputable brands, start-up ventures, and offshore IT companies, helping them realize their digital solutions and delivering effectively, efficiently, and on time.

CulpzLab has worked with a plethora of clients globally. With a diverse technology background, industry expertise, and a client footprint that extends to more than 14 countries, CulpzLab is well positioned to help organizations derive maximum value from their IT investments and fully support their business aims.

CulpzLab's core business purpose is to invent, engineer, and deliver technology solutions that drive business value, create social value, and improve the lives of customers.

> I would like to acknowledge the creators of Unity3D program, the amazing tool that allows the ultimate digital experience in creative expression. I'd also like to thank my clients for being part of the fun! Many of you have become good friends over my creative successes. And finally, I'd like to thank R.K.Rajanjan, who taught me how to love and appreciate technologies.

Ranpariya Ankur J. [PAHeartBeat] represents himself in the gaming world as PAHeartBeat. He has vast experience in the computer programming field from FoxPro to Microsoft .NET technologies. In game programming, he works with one of India's successful game studios, GameAnax Inc., by IndiaNIC InfoTech Ltd., as a Unity3D game programmer, and also works on racing titles for mobile device-based games and studio's internal reusable code "GameAnax Engine", which works in Unity3D for the iOS and Android platforms. He has worked on the two most successful in-house games, *Crazy Monster Truck – Escape* and *Go Karts*, and has also worked on client projects.

Before this, he hasn't worked for any other books either as a reviewer or as a co-author; it's his first experience in book reviewing.

> I would to like to thank my family and my roommates who give me space to work for games at night and adjust their routines and time according to my schedule, thus providing their help.

www.PacktPub.com

Support files, eBooks, discount offers and more

You might want to visit www.PacktPub.com for support files and downloads related to your book.

Did you know that Packt offers eBook versions of every book published, with PDF and ePub files available? You can upgrade to the eBook version at www.PacktPub.com and as a print book customer, you are entitled to a discount on the eBook copy. Get in touch with us at service@packtpub.com for more details.

At www.PacktPub.com, you can also read a collection of free technical articles, sign up for a range of free newsletters and receive exclusive discounts and offers on Packt books and eBooks.

http://PacktLib.PacktPub.com

Do you need instant solutions to your IT questions? PacktLib is Packt's online digital book library. Here, you can access, read and search across Packt's entire library of books.

Why Subscribe?

- Fully searchable across every book published by Packt
- Copy and paste, print and bookmark content
- On demand and accessible via web browser

Free Access for Packt account holders

If you have an account with Packt at www.PacktPub.com, you can use this to access PacktLib today and view nine entirely free books. Simply use your login credentials for immediate access.

Table of Contents

Preface   **1**

**Chapter 1: Introduction to E-Learning and the
Three Cs of 3D Games**   **7**

  Understanding e-learning   **8**

  Introducing our game – Geography Quest   **10**

  Comprehending the three Cs   **11**

  Creating our first scene   **12**

  Developing the character system   **13**

  Building character representation   **14**

  Developing the camera code   **15**

    Implementing GameCam.cs   16

  Developing the player controls code   **21**

    Implementing PlayerControls.cs   21

  Try it out!   **26**

  Summary   **26**

Chapter 2: Interactive Objects and MissionMgr   **27**

  Understanding the base scripts   **28**

  Building an interactive object   **29**

    Implementing the CustomGameObj script   30

    Implementing the InteractiveObj script   31

    Implementing the ObjectInteraction script   33

    Implementing the InventoryItem script   34

    Implementing the InventoryMgr script   36

      Implementing the DisplayInventory method   40

    Implementing the MissionMgr script   44

    Implementing the Mission script   46

    Implementing the MissionToken script   48

    Implementing the SimpleLifespanScript   48

Putting it all together	**49**
Testing the mission system	52
Try it out!	**54**
Summary	**54**
Chapter 3: Mission One – Find the Facts	**55**
Finding the facts	**55**
Designing games to maximize fun	**57**
The teaching loop in game design	**58**
Implementing the core classes for mission one	**58**
Creating a terrain	58
Creating the FlagLocators GameObject	61
Creating the FlagMonument GameObject	61
Creating the MonumentMgr Script	61
Creating the InventoryPlaceOnMonument class	63
Creating the MissionMgrHelper script	63
Creating the TriviaCardScript script	64
Creating the SetupMissionOne script	65
Creating the flag Prefabs	67
Creating the pop-up card Prefabs	70
Creating the mission pop-up Prefab	71
Creating the mission reward Prefabs	72
Creating the FoundAllTheFlags Prefab	72
Creating the ReturnedTheFlagsResult Prefab	73
Configuring the mission manager	74
Playing the level!	75
Summary	**75**
Chapter 4: Mission One – Future Proofing the Code	**77**
Reorganizing our GameObjects in the Scene view	**78**
Creating a global scene	79
Creating a first level scene	80
Adding new scenes to the project	81
Creating the PopupMainMenu GameObject	82
An introduction to Finite State Machines	**84**
Implementing an FSM in a game	85
The switch case FSM	85
Classes implementation of FSM	86
Implementing the GameMgr script	**86**
Reflecting on our code changes	**89**
Analyzing code functionality	**90**
Updating some systems	**91**

Making the ScorePlate active	**92**
Updating the player motion algorithm	**94**
Playing the level!	**95**
Summary	**95**
Chapter 5: User Interfaces in Unity	**97**
Getting familiar with Unity UI classes	**98**
Developing the pop-up system	**98**
Exploring the GUIText component	**99**
Interpreting the members on GUIText	99
Exploring the GUITexture component	**100**
Exploring the TextMesh component	**101**
Ideal use of TextMesh	102
Creating clickable text elements	**102**
Detecting mouse clicks	102
Detecting mouse over	102
Detecting leaving mouse over	102
Exploring UnityScript and the GUIButton object	**103**
Using UnityGUI	103
Creating a clickable button	103
Detecting a mouse click	104
Building the main menu pop up	**104**
Testing our work	**113**
Future extensions	**114**
Summary	**114**
Chapter 6: NPCs and Associated Technology	**115**
Creating the NPC GameObject	**116**
Implementing the npcScript class	116
Implementing the SplineMgr class	**119**
Connecting SplineMgr to NPCScript	**124**
Implementing the NPC decision system	**127**
Implementing the npcCondition script	128
Implementing the npcResponse script	129
Implementing the npcInteraction script	129
Implementing the npcDecisionMgr script	131
Building a collection of NPC conditions and responses	**132**
Implementing the condition_closerThanThresh script	132
Implementing the condition_fartherThanThresh script	133
Implementing the response_changeState script	134
Putting it all together	**135**
Summary	**137**

Chapter 7: Mission Two – Testing a Player's Learning   139
Exploring the structure of mission two   140
Defining the framework for mission two   140
Adding a mission to the missionMgr script   142
Extending the GameCam script   142
Modifying the terrain   143
Adding NpcRacers to the mission   143
Creating the start and finish line flags   145
Creating the LevelStart and LevelFinished pop ups   147
Creating the setupLevel2 Prefab   149
Creating the raceStartup Prefab   150
Implementing the LevelLogicObj GameObject   152
Summary   159

Chapter 8: Adding Animations   161
Exploring 3D hierarchies   161
Skinned meshes in Unity3D   162
Acquiring and importing models   162
Exploring the Mechanim animation system   165
Choosing appropriate animations   166
Building a simple character animation FSM   166
Exploring in-place versus root motion animation   170
Adding the character script   171
Building a zombie racer animation FSM   172
Building a quiz racer animation FSM   174
Exploring the Unity animation editor   177
Summary   179

Chapter 9: Synthesis of Knowledge   181
Understanding the mission three GameObjects   182
Applying learning theory to mission three   183
Creating the structure for mission three   184
Modifying the terrain   184
Adding visitors to the park   185
Modifying the pop-up system   185
Creating the NpcLocators Prefab   186
Creating the CorrectResponse Prefabs   187
Modifying the quiz cards   187
Adding another data condition   189
Using the setupLevel3 Prefab   189
Creating the AddScore condition   191
Creating the ShowLevel3Results response   192

Creating the Time object	**193**
Modifying the LevelLogicObj object	**196**
Rewarding the player	**197**
Summary	**199**
Chapter 10: An Extensible Game Framework Pattern in Unity	**201**
Load additively	**202**
Using delete/load patterns	**203**
Refactoring our work	**204**
The pop-up system	204
Updating level 3 pop ups	205
Updating level 2 pop ups	207
Updating level 1 pop ups	208
Refactoring level 2	**210**
Implementing a system to connect object references	**211**
Updating the SetupMission2 script	214
Refactoring level 3	**216**
Playing and distributing your game	**219**
Reflecting on e-learning and game design	**220**
Summary	**221**
Index	**223**

Preface

E-learning can be described as the use of computers and digital technology to facilitate teaching and learning. One popular method of accomplishing this, and which is also the approach we will take in this book, is through gamification of learning, that is, the application of cognitive psychology and game-based rules to learning systems.

At the time of writing this book, it is projected that by the year 2020, 85 percent of all daily human tasks will be gamified to some extent (*Everyone is a Gamer*, a HTML document by Corcione, Andrew, and Fran Tardo, available at `www.prnewswire.com`, February 25, 2014. This document was accessed on February 28, 2014, `http://www.prnewswire.com/news-releases/everyones-a-gamer---ieee-experts-predict-gaming-will-be-integrated-into-more-than-85-percent-of-daily-tasks-by-2020-247100431.html`). This book was written in parts to address the need of young programmers to have a robust and substantial example of an e-learning game to learn from.

The reader will participate in the development of an e-learning game that teaches American geography, Geography Quest. The code and the book were written in tandem so that the text could serve as an accompanying guide to the software.

What this book covers

Chapter 1, Introduction to E-Learning and the Three Cs of 3D Games, introduces e-learning and how games are effective at targeting learning outcomes. It also introduces us to Unity3D and guides us through the development of the character, camera, and control systems for the game.

Chapter 2, Interactive Objects and MissionMgr, helps us to develop some of the core technology for our game foundation. We will implement a system that tracks the user's progress in the game through the concept of a mission. We also develop an interactive object class the player can interact with.

Chapter 3, Mission One – Find the Facts, helps us to code the first level of our game by applying the learning theory we know and the technology we have developed to create an exploration level.

Chapter 4, Mission One – Future Proofing the Code, helps us finish developing the first level of our game after taking a look back at our design needs and refactoring our code so that it is maintainable and extendible. This level presents the learning outcomes to the player for the first time.

Chapter 5, User Interfaces in Unity, takes a sojourn into user interface technology in Unity. We then apply our knowledge and develop a pop-up windows system that will be used in our game.

Chapter 6, NPCs and Associated Technology, helps us apply the technology we have already built in the creation of simple computer-controlled characters for our game.

Chapter 7, Mission Two – Testing a Player's Learning, guides us to develop the second level of our game, applying all of the systems and technology we have developed thus far. This level of the game gives the player an opportunity to manipulate and practice the learning outcomes.

Chapter 8, Adding Animations, takes another sojourn into the various animation systems in Unity3D. We then apply this knowledge by replacing our existing characters with 3D animated models.

Chapter 9, Synthesis of Knowledge, helps us to develop the last level of our game in this chapter by using all of the technology and theory we have learned. This level of the game challenges the user to master the desired learning outcomes.

Chapter 10, An Extensible Game Framework Pattern in Unity, integrates our game levels into one extensible framework. We will polish it more and then package the game up for your user to run on their PC.

What you need for this book

You will need Unity Version 4.2.2f1, which at the time of writing this book may be downloaded from `http://unity3d.com/unity/download/archive`.

Who this book is for

This book is intended for beginners in Unity3D programming who wish to develop games in Unity3D that teach and inform the user of specific learning outcomes. Common target applications could be for training games that teach procedures at the workplace, for teaching policies or best practices, or for factual learning in the classroom. While some familiarity with C# and some programming concepts would be beneficial, it is not mandatory.

Conventions

In this book, you will find a number of styles of text that distinguish between different kinds of information. Here are some examples of these styles, and an explanation of their meaning.

Code words in text, database table names, folder names, filenames, file extensions, pathnames, dummy URLs, user input, and Twitter handles are shown as follows: "The Hat object will serve as a visual cue for us in this chapter as we refine the controls and camera code."

A block of code is set as follows:

```
Public float height;
Public float desiredDistance;
Public float heightDamp;
Public float rotDamp;
```

New terms and **important words** are shown in bold. Words that you see on the screen, in menus or dialog boxes for example, appear in the text like this: "Under **Edit | Render Settings**, go to the **Skybox Material** panel of the **Inspector** pane, and add one of the skybox materials from the skybox package."

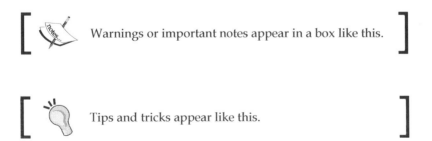

Warnings or important notes appear in a box like this.

Tips and tricks appear like this.

Reader feedback

Feedback from our readers is always welcome. Let us know what you think about this book—what you liked or may have disliked. Reader feedback is important for us to develop titles that you really get the most out of.

To send us general feedback, simply send an e-mail to feedback@packtpub.com, and mention the book title via the subject of your message.

If there is a topic that you have expertise in and you are interested in either writing or contributing to a book, see our author guide on www.packtpub.com/authors.

Customer support

Now that you are the proud owner of a Packt book, we have a number of things to help you to get the most from your purchase.

Downloading the example code

You can download the example code files for all Packt books you have purchased from your account at http://www.packtpub.com. If you purchased this book elsewhere, you can visit http://www.packtpub.com/support and register to have the files e-mailed directly to you.

Downloading the color images of this book

We also provide you a PDF file that has color images of the screenshots/diagrams used in this book. The color images will help you better understand the changes in the output. You can download this file from: http://www.packtpub.com/sites/default/files/downloads/3424OS_Images.pdf

Errata

Although we have taken every care to ensure the accuracy of our content, mistakes do happen. If you find a mistake in one of our books—maybe a mistake in the text or the code—we would be grateful if you would report this to us. By doing so, you can save other readers from frustration and help us improve subsequent versions of this book. If you find any errata, please report them by visiting http://www.packtpub.com/submit-errata, selecting your book, clicking on the **errata submission form** link, and entering the details of your errata. Once your errata are verified, your submission will be accepted and the errata will be uploaded on our website, or added to any list of existing errata, under the Errata section of that title. Any existing errata can be viewed by selecting your title from http://www.packtpub.com/support.

Piracy

Piracy of copyright material on the Internet is an ongoing problem across all media. At Packt, we take the protection of our copyright and licenses very seriously. If you come across any illegal copies of our works, in any form, on the Internet, please provide us with the location address or website name immediately so that we can pursue a remedy.

Please contact us at copyright@packtpub.com with a link to the suspected pirated material.

We appreciate your help in protecting our authors, and our ability to bring you valuable content.

Questions

You can contact us at questions@packtpub.com if you are having a problem with any aspect of the book, and we will do our best to address it.

1
Introduction to E-Learning and the Three Cs of 3D Games

In this chapter, we will start developing a 3D e-learning game. To illustrate the concept of e-learning in games, our game will teach players American state flags and trivia over the course of three levels. After beginning with a definition of e-learning games and how they relate to "traditional" video games, we will carry on with implementing the core systems that control the main character of the game and define its abilities and ways to control the camera that follows the player in our 3D world.

In this chapter, we will cover the following topics:

- Understanding e-learning
- Introducing our game—Geography Quest
- Comprehending the three Cs
- Creating our first scene
- Developing the character system
- Building character representation
- Developing code for the camera
- Developing code for the player controls

Understanding e-learning

Broadly speaking, e-learning is the use of digital technology to facilitate learning. This could include Internet servers and web browsers to deliver course material online in an asynchronous way. It could include the use of embedded videos in an application that a user can review at his or her leisure in bite-sized chunks. For our purposes in this book, we will focus on the gamification of learning and the use of multimedia and game software to deliver our specific learning outcomes.

The reasons that gamification works in e-learning are varied and are supported by both traditional pedagogy and neurobiology. We list, in no particular order, some of the most compelling reasons as follows:

- **Immersion**: Games that are immersive to the player naturally activate more meaningful learning pathways in the brain. This is because the brain stores and consolidates different types of information in different regions of the brain, based on their relevance. By tying in a strong cinematic experience to the delivery of learning outcomes, you can recruit these systems in the user's brain to learn and retain the material you want to deliver.

    - But how do we make our games immersive? From the body of knowledge in movie, TV, and consumer game development, there are many design features we could borrow. However, to pick two important ones, we know that good character development and camera work are large contributors to the immersion level of a story.

    - Character development occurs when the view or opinion of the main character changes in the eye of the player. This happens naturally in a story when the main character participates in a journey that changes or evolves his or her world view, stature, or status. This evolution almost always happens as a result of a problem that occurs in the story. We will borrow from this principle as we plan the obstacles for our player to overcome.

    - Cinematic camera work helps encourage immersion because the more interesting and dramatic the view of the world that the player experiences, the more actively does the player engage with the story, and hence the learning outcomes by association.

    - Along with cinematic camera work, we must be sure to balance the playability of the game. Ironically, it is often the case that the more playable the game camera is, the less cinematic it is!

- **Spatial learning**: It is worth giving spatial learning a special mention despite its close association to immersion as a modality of learning. It is known that a specific area of the brain stores the mental map of where things are in your surroundings. Games that have a spatial navigation component to them naturally will recruit this part of the brain to facilitate learning.

- **Active learning**: Instruction is passive and learning is active! Playing games that require levels of thought beyond passive observation are naturally more conducive to learning and retention. By using games that have challenges and puzzles, we force the player to participate in higher order thinking while manipulating the subject matter of the learning outcomes.

- **Reinforcement and conditioning**: Psychologists and learning professionals know that, for a given scenario, positive reinforcement of good behavior increases the likelihood of eliciting the same good behavior the next time that scenario presents itself. Traditional game designers know this lesson very well, as they reward the player both quantitatively (with points and items and power-ups and in-game related collectibles). They also reward the player qualitatively by inducing visceral reactions that feel good. These include being rewarded with on-screen particle effects, visually appealing cut scenes, explosions, sound effects, on screen animation, and so on. Slot machine developers know this lesson well as they play sounds and animations that elicit a feel-good response and reward payouts that condition the player to engage in the positive behavior of playing the game.

- **Emotional attachment**: Games that build an emotional attachment in their players are more likely to garner active play and attention from their users. This results in higher retention of the learning objectives. But how do you engineer attachment into a design? One way is the use of avatars. It turns out that, as the player controls a character in the game, guides his or her actions, customizes his or her appearance, and otherwise invests time and energy in it, he or she may build an attachment to the avatar as it can become an extension of the player's self.

- **Cognitive flow**: Have you ever participated in a task and lost track of time? Psychologists call this the state of flow, and it is known that in this heightened state of engagement, the brain is working at its best and learning potential is increased. We try and encourage the player to enter a state of flow in e-learning games by providing an immersive experience as well by asking the player to complete tasks that are challenging, interesting, and in scenarios with just enough emotional pressure or excitation to keep it interesting.

- **Safe practice environment**: Video games and real-time simulations are good training vehicles because they are inherently safe. The player can practice a skill inside a game without any risk of bodily harm by repeating it in a virtual environment; this enables the player to experience freedom from physical repercussions and encourages exploration and active learning.

An astute reader may ask "What is the difference between e-learning games and consumer games?". This is a good question, which we would answer with "the learning outcomes themselves". A consumer game aims to teach the player how to play the game, how to master the mechanics, how to navigate the levels, and so on. An e-learning game uses the same design principles as consumer games, with the primary goal of achieving retention of the learning outcomes.

Introducing our game – Geography Quest

In our e-learning game, Geography Quest, we will follow the adventures of the player as park ranger, as you clean up the park to find the missing flags, participate in a trivia challenge/race, and then ultimately patrol your park helping the visitors with their questions. Through each chapter we not only build and extend our technology built inside Unity3D to achieve the design needs of this game, but we also apply the design considerations discussed earlier to develop compelling and effective e-learning content.

Our game will implement the following design features of an effective e-learning game:

- Immersion
- Spatial learning
- Active learning
- Reinforcement and conditioning
- Emotional attachment
- Cognitive flow
- A safe practice environment

Comprehending the three Cs

To design the software for the user experience in a 3D game, we can break the problem down into three systems: the camera, the character, and the controls. In this chapter, we will build the foundation of our e-learning game by developing the framework for these components:

- **Camera**: This system is responsible for the virtual cinematography in the game. It ensures that the avatar is always on screen, that the relevant aspects of the 3D world are shown, and that this experience is achieved in a dynamic, interesting, and responsive way.

- **Character**. This is the avatar itself. It is a 3D model of the personification of the player that is under direct user control. The character must represent the hero as well as possess the functional attributes necessary for the learning objectives.

- **Controls**. This system refers to the control layer that the user interacts within the game. The genre and context of the game can and should affect how this system behaves. This system is impacted by the hardware that is available to the user to interact with. There are potentially many different input hardware devices we could choose to program for; while we may encounter gamepads, touch pads and touchscreens, and motion tracking cameras on potential target PCs, we will focus our attention on the traditional keyboard and mouse for input in our example.

These three systems are tightly coupled and are the trinity of the core 3D gameplay experience. Throughout a normal video game development cycle, we as game programmers may find ourselves making multiple iterations on these three systems until they "feel right". This is normal and is to be expected; however, the impact of changes in one system on the other two cannot be underestimated.

Creating our first scene

With these requirements in mind, let's build the framework:

1. Create a plane, positioned at (0,0,0), and name it ground.

2. Under **Edit | Render Settings**, go to the **Skybox Material** panel of the **Inspector** pane, and add one of the skybox materials from the skybox package.

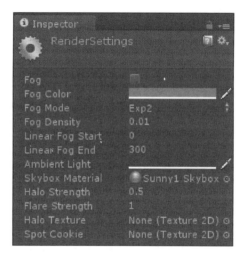

3. The **GameObject** drop-down menu is where you can select different types of basic Unity3D objects to populate your world. Create a directional light to the scene from **GameObject | Create Other**, and place it at (0,10,0) for readability. Set its orientation to something like (50, 330, 0) to achieve a neat shading effect on the player capsule. In our world, the y axis will mean "in the air" and the x and z axes will correspond to the horizontal plane of the world.

Congratulations! You have created the testbed for this chapter. Now let's add the character system.

Developing the character system

The character system is responsible for making the avatar of the game look and respond appropriately. It is crucial to get this right in an e-learning game because studies show that player attachment and engagement correlate to how well the player relates or personalizes with the hero. In later chapters, we will learn about how to do this with animation and player customization.

For now, our character system needs to allow coarse interactions with the environment (ground plane). To do this, we shall now create the following avatar capsule:

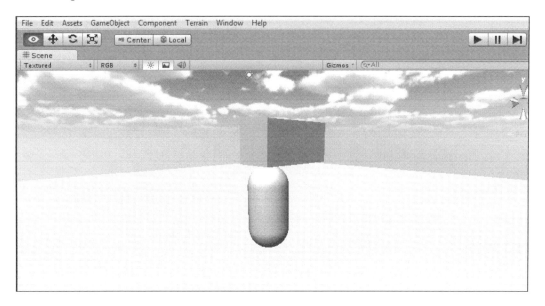

Building character representation

With these requirements in mind, let's build the framework:

1. From **GameObject | CreateOther**, select **Capsule**, and place it at (0, 2.5, 0), as shown in the following screenshot:

2. Name the capsule `Player` in the **Inspector** pane.

3. Create a cube in a similar fashion, and parent it to the capsule by dragging it onto the hero. Scale it to (0.5,0.5,2), and set its local position to (0,1.5,0.5).

4. Name the cube object `Hat`.

Congratulations! You now have a representation of our hero in the game. The `Hat` object will serve as a visual cue for us in this chapter as we refine the controls and camera code.

Developing the camera code

In our 3D game, the main camera mode will follow a third-person algorithm. This means that it will follow the player from behind, trying to keep the player on screen and centered in view at all times. Before we start developing the camera, we need to think about the basic requirements of our game in order to be able to program the camera to achieve good cinematographic results. This list of requirements will grow over time; however, by considering the requirements early on, we build an extensible system throughout the course of this book by applying good system design in our software. In no particular order, we list the requirements of a good camera system as follows:

- It needs to be able to track the hero at a pleasing distance and speed and in an organic way

- It needs to be able to transition in an appealing way, from tracking various objects

- It needs to be able to frame objects in the field of view, in a cinematic and pleasing way

Starting with an initial camera and motion system based on the Unity3D examples, we will extend these over time. We do this not only because it is instructive but also with the aim of extending them and making them our own over time. With these requirements in mind, let's build the camera code. Before we do, let's consider some pseudocode for the algorithm.

Implementing GameCam.cs

The GameCam script is the class that we will attach our MainCamera object to; it will be responsible for the motion of our in-game camera and for tracking the player on screen. The following five steps describe our GameCam camera algorithm:

1. For every frame that our camera updates, if we have a valid trackObj GameObject reference, do the following:

    1. Cache the facing angle and the height of the object we are tracking.

    2. Cache the current facing angle and height of the camera (the GameObject that this script is attached to).

2. Linearly interpolate from current facing to desired facing according to a dampening factor.

3. Linearly interpolate from current height to desired height according to another dampening factor.

4. Place the camera behind the track object, at the interpolated angle, facing the track object so that the object of interest can be seen in view, as shown in the following screenshot:

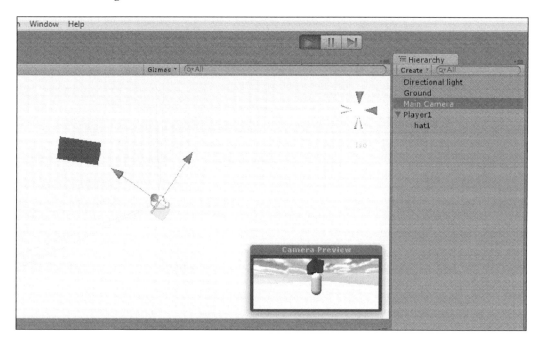

Now let's implement this algorithm in C# code by performing the following steps:

1. Right click on the `Chapter1 assets` folder and select **Create New C# Script**. Name it `GameCam` and add it to the `Main Camera` object.

2. Create a public `GameObject` reference called `TrackObj` with the following code. This will point to the `GameObject` that this camera is tracking at any given time, as shown in the following code:

    ```
    public GameObject trackObj;
    ```

3. Create the following four public float variables that will allow adjustment of the camera behavior in the object inspector. We will leave these uninitialized and then find working default values with the inspector, as shown in the following code:

    ```
    Public float height;
    Public float desiredDistance;
    Public float heightDamp;
    Public float rotDamp;
    ```

    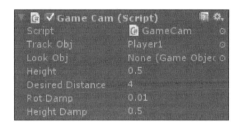

4. Recall that the `Update()` loop of any GameObject gets called repeatedly while the game simulation is running, which makes this method a great candidate in which we can put our main camera logic. Hence, inside the `Update()` loop of this script, we will call a `UpdateRotAndTrans()` custom method, which will contain the actual camera logic. We will place this logic inside the `UpdateRotAndTrans()` method. This method will update the rotation (facing angle) and translation (position) of the camera in the world; this is how `GameCam` will accomplish the stated goal of moving in the world and tracking the player:

    ```
    void Update() {
      UpdateRotAndTrans();
    }
    ```

5. Above the update loop, let's implement the `UpdateRotAndTrans()` method as follows:

```
void UpdateRotAndTrans () {
  // to be filled in
}
```

6. Inside this method, step 1 of our algorithm is accomplished with a sanity check on `trackObj`. By checking for null and reporting an error to `debugLog`, we can make catching bugs much easier by looking at the console. This is shown in the following code:

```
if (trackObj) {
}
else {
  Debug.Log("GameCamera:Error,trackObj invalid");
}
```

7. Step 2 of our algorithm is to store the desired rotation and height in two local float variables. In the case of the height, we offset the height of `trackObj` by an exposed global variable `height` so that we can adjust the specifics of the object as shown in the following code (sometimes an object may have its transform 0 at the ground plane, which would not look pleasing, we need numbers to tweak):

```
DesiredRotationAngle = trackObj.transform.eulerAngles.y;
DesiredHeight = trackObj.transform.position.y + height;
```

8. We also need to store the local variants of the preceding code for processing in our algorithm. Note the simplified but similar code compared to the code in the previous step. Remember that the `this` pointer is implied if we don't explicitly place it in front of a component (such as `transform`):

```
float RotAngle = transform.eulerAngles.y;
float Height = transform.position.y;
```

9. Step 3 of our algorithm is where we do the actual **LERP (linear interpolation)** of the current and destination values for y-axis rotation and height. Remember that making use of the LERP method between two values means having to calculate a series of new values between the start and end that differs between one another by a constant amount.

Remember that Euler angles are the rotation about the cardinal axes, and Euler *y* indicates the horizontal angle of the object. Since these values change, we smooth out the current rotation and height more with a smaller dampening value, and we tighten the interpolation with a larger value.

Also note that we multiply `heightDamp` by `Time.deltaTime` in order to make the height interpolation frame rate independent, and instead dependent on elapsed time, as follows:

```
RotAngle = Mathf.LerpAngle
(RotAngle, DesiredRotationAngle, rotDamp);
Height = Mathf.Lerp
(Height, DesiredHeight, heightDamp * Time.deltaTime);
```

10. The fourth and last step in our `GameCam` algorithm is to compute the position of the camera.

    Now that we have an interpolated rotation and height, we will place the camera behind `trackObject` at the interpolated height and angle. To do this, we will take the facing vector of `trackObject` and scale it by the negative value of `desiredDistance` to find a vector pointing in the opposite direction to `trackObject`; doing this requires us to convert `eulerAngles` to `Quaternion` to simplify the math (we can do it with one API function!).

    Adding this to the `trackObject` position and setting the height gives the desired offset behind the object, as shown in the following code:

```
Quaternion CurrentRotation = Quaternion.Euler
(0.0f, RotAngle, 0.0f);
Vector3 pos = trackObj.transform.position;
pos -=
CurrentRotation * Vector3.forward * desiredDistance;
pos.y = Height;
transform.position = pos;
```

11. As a final step, we point the `LookAt` GameObject reference of the camera to the center of `trackObject` so that it is always precisely in the middle of the field of view. It is most important to never lose the object you are tracking in a 3D game. This is critical!

```
transform.LookAt (trackObj.transform.position);
```

Congratulations! We have now written our first `camera` class that can smoothly track a rotating and translating object. To test this class, let's set the following default values in the **Inspector** pane as seen in the previous screenshot:

- **TrackObj**: Set this to the **Player1** object by dragging-and-dropping the object reference from the **Hierarchy** tab to the `trackObj` reference in the object inspector.

- **Height**: Set this to `0.25`. In general, the lower the camera, the more dramatic the effect but the less playable the game will be (because the user can see less of the world on screen).

- **Desired Distance**: Set this to `4`. At this setting, we can see the character framed nicely on screen when it is both moving and standing still.

- **Rot Damp**: Set this to `0.01`. The smaller this value, the looser and more interesting the rotation effect. The larger this value, the more tense the spring in the interpolation.

- **Height Damp**: Set this to `0.5`. The smaller this value, the looser and more interesting the height blending effect.

Once the player controls are developed (refer to the next section), try experimenting with these values and see what happens.

Developing the player controls code

The third system we need to implement is the controls or how the character will
respond to the user input. As a first pass, we need to be able to move our player in
the world, so we will implement walk forward, walk backwards, walk left, and walk
right. Luckily for us, Unity gives us an input system with axes so that we can write
our control code once, and it will work with any devices that have an axis (such
as keyboard or joypad). Of course, the devil is in the detail and keyboard controls
behave differently from joypads, so we will write our code for keyboard input as it
is the most responsive and most ubiquitous device. Once this script is finished, its
behavior in combination with the GameCam script will control how the player motion
feels in the game.

Implementing PlayerControls.cs

For every frame our player updates, perform the following steps that describe our
PlayeControls algorithm:

1. Store the forward and right vectors of the current camera.

2. Store the raw axis input from the controller (keyboard or joystick). These
   values will range from -1.0 to 1.0, corresponding to full left or right, or full
   forward or backwards. Note that if you use a joystick, the rate of change of
   these values will generally be much slower than if a keyboard is used, so the
   code that processes it must be adjusted accordingly.

3. Apply the raw input to transform the current camera basis vectors and
   compute a camera relative target direction vector.

4. Interpolate the current movement vector towards the target vector and damp
   the rate of change of the movement vector, storing the result away.

5. Compute the displacement of the camera with *movement * movespeed* and
   apply this to the camera.

6. Rotate the camera to the current move direction vector.

Now let's implement this algorithm in C# code:

1. Right click on the `Chapter1 assets` folder and select **Create New C# Script**. Name it `PlayerControls.cs`. Add this script to `GameObject` of **Player1** by dragging-and-dropping it onto the object.

2. Add a `CharacterController` component to the player's `GameObject` component as well. If Unity asks you whether you want to replace the box collider, agree to the change.

3. Create `public Vector3 moveDirection` that will be used to store the current actual direction vector of the player. We initialize it to the zero vector by default as follows:

    ```
    public Vector3 moveDirection = Vector3.zero;
    ```

4. Create three public float variables: `rotateSpeed`, `moveSpeed`, and `speedSmoothing`. The first two are coefficients of motion for rotation and translation, and the third is a factor that influences the smoothing of `moveSpeed`. Note that `moveSpeed` is private because this will only be computed as the result of the smoothing calculation between `moveDirection` and `targetDirection` as shown in the following code:

    ```
    public Float rotateSpeed;
    private float moveSpeed = 0.0f;
    public float speedSmoothing = 10.0f;
    ```

5. Inside the update loop of this script, we will call a custom method called `UpdateMovement()`. This method will contain the code that actually reads input from the user and moves the player in the game as shown in the following code:

    ```
    void Update() {
      UpdateMovement()
    }
    ```

6. Above the update loop, let's implement the `UpdateMovement()` method as follows:

    ```
    void UpdateMovement () {
      // to be filled in
    }
    ```

7. Inside this method, step 1 is accomplished by storing the horizontal projection of the forward and right vectors of the current camera as follows:

    ```
    Vector3 cameraForward = Camera.mainCamera.transform.
    TransformDirection
    (Vector3.forward);
    ```

8. We project onto the horizontal plane because we want the character's motion to be parallel to the horizontal plane rather than vary with the camera's angle. We also use `Normalize` to ensure that the vector is well formed, as shown in the following code:

```
cameraForward.y = 0.0f;
cameraForward.Normalize();
```

Also, note the trick whereby we find the right vector by flipping the x and z components and negating the last component. This is faster than extracting and transforming the right vector, but returns the same result shown in the following code:

```
Vector3 cameraRight = new Vector3
(cameraForward.z, 0.0f, -cameraForward.x);
```

9. We store the raw axis values from Unity's `Input` class. Recall that this is the class that handles input for us, from which we can poll button and axes values. For h (which has a range from -1 to 1), the value between this range corresponds to an amount of horizontal displacement on the analog stick, joystick, or a keypress, as shown in the following code:

```
float v = Input.GetAxisRaw("Vertical");
```

For v (which ranges from -1 to 1), the value between this range corresponds to an amount of vertical displacement of the analog stick, joystick, or a different keypress.

```
float h = Input.GetAxisRaw("Horizontal");
```

To see the keybindings, please check the input class settings under **Edit | ProjectSettings | Input**. There, under the **Axes** field in the object inspector, we can see all of the defined axes in the input manager class, their bindings, their names, and their parameters.

1. We compute the target direction vector for the character as proportional to the user input (v, h). By transforming (v, h) into camera space, the result is a world space vector that holds a camera relative motion vector that we store in `targetDirection` as shown in the following code:

```
Vector3 targetDirection =
  h * cameraRight + v * cameraForward;
```

2. If this target vector is non-zero (when the user is moving, and hence v, h are non-zero), we update `moveDirection` by rotating it smoothly (and by a small magnitude), towards `moveTarget`. By doing this in every frame, the actual direction eventually approximates the target direction, even as `targetDirection` itself changes.

We keep `moveDirection` normalized because our move speed calculation assumes a unit direction vector as shown in the following code:

```
moveDirection = Vector3.RotateTowards
(moveDirection, targetDirection, rotateSpeed * Mathf.Deg2Rad *
Time.deltaTime, 1000);
moveDirection = moveDirection.normalized;
```

3. We smoothly LERP the speed of our character up and down, trailing the actual magnitude of the `targetDirection` vector. This is to create an appealing effect that reduces jitter in the player and is crucial when we are using keyboard controls, where the variance in v and h raw data is at its highest, as shown in the following code:

```
float curSmooth =
speedSmoothing * Time.deltaTime;
float targetSpeed = Mathf.Min
(targetDirection.magnitude, 1.0f);
moveSpeed = Mathf.Lerp
(moveSpeed, targetSpeed, curSmooth);
```

4. We compute the displacement vector for the player in this frame with *movementDirection * movespeed* (remember that `movespeed` is smoothly interpolated and `moveDirection` is smoothly rotated toward `targetDirecton`).

    We scale displacement by `Time.delta` time (the amount of real time that has elapsed since the last frame). We do this so that our calculation is time dependent rather than frame rate dependent as shown in the following code:

```
Vector3 displacement =
moveDirection * moveSpeed * Time.deltaTime;
```

5. Then, we move the character by invoking the `move` method on the `CharacterController` component of the player, passing the `displacement` vector as a parameter as follows:

```
this.GetComponent<CharacterController>()
.Move(displacement);
```

6. Finally, we assign the rotation of `MoveDirection` to the rotation of the transform as follows:

```
transform.rotation = Quaternion.LookRotation (moveDirection);
```

Congratulations! You have now written your first player controls class that can read user input from multiple axes and use that to drive a rotating and translating character capsule. To test this class, let's set the following default values in the **Inspector** pane as seen in the previous screenshot:

- **Track Obj**: Set this to the **Player1** object by dragging-and-dropping the object reference from the **Hierarchy** tab to the trackObj reference in the object inspector.
- **Height**: Set this to 0.25. In general, the lower the camera, the more dramatic the effect, but the less playable the game will be (because the user can see less of the world on screen).
- **Desired Distance**: Set this to 4. At this setting, we can see the character framed nicely on screen when it is both moving and standing still.
- **Rot Damp**: Set this to 0.01. The smaller this value, the looser and more interesting the rotation effect. The larger this value, the more tense the spring in the interpolation.
- **Height Damp**: Set this to 0.5. The smaller this value, the looser and more interesting the height blending effect.

Try experimenting with the following values and see what happens:

- **Rotate Speed** : Set the default to 100. The higher the value, the faster the player will rotate when the horizontal axis is set to full left or right.
- **Speed Smoothing**: Set the default to 10. The higher this value, the smoother the character's acceleration and deceleration.

Try experimenting with these values to understand their effect on the player's motion behavior.

Try it out!

Test your "Three C" framework by debugging the game in the editor. Press play and then adjust the parameters on the **PlayerControls** and **GameCam** script to tighten or loosen the controls to your liking. Once you have a set of parameters that works for you, make sure to save your scene and project.

Summary

We learned about the three Cs in core gameplay experience programming. We developed base systems for the character, controls, and camera that have parameters so that designers and programmers can adjust the look and feel of the game quickly and easily.

Going forward, we will build the code necessary to make our game interactive! We will learn how to program interactive objects in our game, and we will develop the technology for a mission system, which will allow the game designer to build missions and objectives, track their status, and give them to the user in a systemic way.

2
Interactive Objects and MissionMgr

A well-designed and engaging e-learning game will challenge the user, track his or her progress, and reward his or her performance appropriately. To do this, a series of classes will be required that will separate what we are tracking with the way in which we interact with it.

We will develop a system to implement a generic object that the user can interact with and collect. We will also develop another system that lets us build an abstract learning objective for the user to accomplish. We will then develop a system to collect objects into an inventory that can be used by the player. Lastly, we will develop software that tracks the user's progress towards these objectives and rewards him or her appropriately for success.

In this chapter, we will cover the following topics:

- Understanding the base scripts
- Building an interactive object
- Putting it all together
- Try it out!
- Summary

Understanding the base scripts

The interactive `Object` class is the base script that enables a player in our game to have meaningful gameplay interactions. To meet the design needs of our game, this script provides an interface with which the game designer can specify how the player will interact with an object as it is picked up. In addition to this, it also permits subtle rotation on the object for a nice effect. The `CustomGameObj` and `ObjectInteraction` helper classes are used by the `object` class to define the specific nature of the interactions and how the object behaves in the inventory when collected.

The `MissionMgr` class is the system that tracks the user's progress through the game and rewards him or her on achieving success. When a user interacts with an interactive object, `MissionToken` attached to it (if any) is collected and tracked by `MissionMgr`. The `MissionMgr` class has a template of all missions, the tokens that each mission is composed of, and the reward that should be given when a mission is satisfied. When the `MissionMgr` class determines that a mission is complete and that all of the tokens from that mission have been collected, it gives a reward to the user.

Lastly, `InventoryMgr` is the system that handles the display of the interactive objects that have been collected. If an object is permitted to be collected, it will be added to the inventory according to its `CustomGameObj` and then displayed in the inventory at the bottom of the screen.

The following list outlines the classes that we will develop in this chapter:

- `CustomGameObj`: This class contains the basic data about an object in our game. It holds the object's name and type. This information will be used when we interact with this object.

- `InteractiveObj`: This class controls the behavior of an object that the user will physically interact with in the game world. It makes the object rotate and also detects when the player gets close enough to it to start an interaction.

- `InventoryMgr`: This class tracks which interactive objects the user has collected. It will also display them in the inventory at the bottom of the screen. Objects can be either unique or can accumulate based on their type.

- `ObjectInteraction`: This class describes how an interactive object should behave and what will be the nature of interaction when the user interacts with it. To start, we will use the `OnCloseEnough` event to dispatch a *collect and put into inventory* interaction.

- `SimpleLifespanScript`: This class is used by the reward objects that are spawned when a mission is complete. This makes them disappear after a predetermined amount of time.

- `MissionToken`: This class represents an abstract logical component of a mission or an objective. These will be collected in ways similar to inventory objects.

- `Mission`: This class represents a collection of mission tokens. When the player obtains all of the tokens, the learning objective will be deemed satisfied.

- `MissionMgr`: This class stores all of the missions currently accessible to the user. It will validate each mission to determine if the player has acquired all of the tokens. If so, it will handle the task of giving the user an appropriate reward for their performance.

The `CustomGameObj` and `InteractiveObj` systems will interact with one another because our game's collecting mechanism is based on how the user primarily acquires and interacts with mission objectives. Once we have this core mechanism coded, with a couple of simple collection missions, we will illustrate how it works:

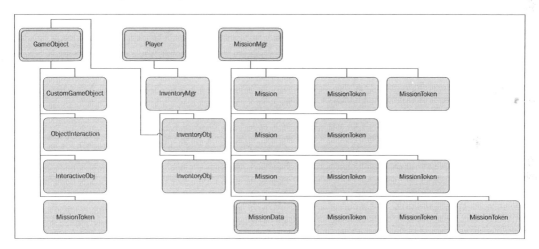

Building an interactive object

With these requirements in mind, let's build the framework for an interactive object that can be collected by the player.

Implementing the CustomGameObj script

We will begin with the `CustomGameObj` class. This class allows us to specify how an interactive object will behave when placed in the inventory, by giving it a unique type that is relevant for our game. Create the script by performing the following steps:

1. Start from the codebase built in *Chapter 1, Introduction to E-Learning and the Three Cs of 3D Games*, to create a new subfolder in the `assets` folder named `Chapter 2`.

2. Using the new script wizard, right-click on it and create a new C# script named `CustomGameObject`.

3. We will also add a public enumerated type to this class called `CustomObjectType`. If you recall, an enumeration is just a list of identifiers of the integer type that share a common logical relationship with one another, such as the types of an object! Not only will this make discerning the type of this object easy to read in the code, but it also serves as an interface to describe the classification of this object. We will use this information to determine some custom rules while adding GameObjects to the inventory. To begin, we will start with a few different types of objects, where an object of the `Coin` type will accumulate in the same slot in the inventory. This holds true for objects of the type `Ruby`, `Diamond`, and so on as well. Unique objects will be added in their own slot in `InventoryMgr` as follows:

```
Public enum CustomObjectType
{
    Invalid = -1,
    Unique = 0,
    Coin = 1,
    Ruby = 2,
    Emerald = 3,
    Diamond = 4

}
```

4. A variable of the `CustomObject` type is added to this class to store the current type from the set discussed in the previous step. We use the `public` keyword so that a user can directly set the value of this variable inside the Unity Editor on an instance of the object:

```
public CustomObjectTypeobjectType CustomObjectType objectType;
```

5. A public variable of the `string` type is added so that Unity users can add some descriptive text to the object while designing them, as shown in the following code; this can be very helpful while debugging or trying to identify the objects inside the editor:

```
public string displayName;
```

6. Declare a method named `validate()`, which will be used to assign the `unnamed_object` string to the `displayName` field if one has not been assigned in the editor, as shown in the following code:

```
public void validate()
{
  if (displayName == "")
    displayName = "unnamed_object";
}
```

Congratulations! We now have a container for the `CustomGameObject` information that our inventory system will use. To continue, let's create the `InteractiveObj` script.

Implementing the InteractiveObj script

The `InteractiveObj` script declares a class that enables simple animation and permits player interactions. Perform the following steps to create the script:

1. To use the new script wizard, right-click inside the `Chapter2` folder of the **Project** tab and add a C# script named `InteractiveObj`.

2. To enable our interactive object to rotate about its own axis at a user specified rate, we need to add two parameters: a rotation axis and a rotation speed, as shown in the following code:

```
public Vector3 rotAxis;
public float rotSpeed;
```

3. We will add a private reference to the `customGameObject` component for this `GameObject` so that we don't have to look it up at runtime. This can be done with the following line of code:

```
private customGameObject gameObjectInfo;
```

4. We will also add an `ObjectInteraction` member variable. This will be the code that specifies what will happen to our `gameObject` when the player interacts with it. There may be many interactions that an interactive object can implement; we will start our example with `OnCloseEnough` and will complete this in the `OnTriggerEnter` method, as shown in the following code:

    ```
    public objectInteraction OnCloseEnough;
    ```

5. In the `Start()` method, we will search for the `CustomGameObject` component attached to `gameObject`. If it is found, we will store the reference in the `gameObjectInfo` private variable. Remember to always check that `gameObjectInfo` is not null so that debugging the code is a straightforward process, as shown in the following code:

    ```
    gameObjectInfo = this.gameObject.GetComponent<customGameObject>();
      if (gameObjectInfo)
        gameObjectInfo.validate();
    ```

6. In the `Update()` method, we will apply a simple rotation to the object around the specified `rotAxis` parameter. We will rotate the object with the speed given in `rotSpeed` multiplied by `Time.deltaTime` so that the number of rotations is a function of the elapsed time rather than the frame time, as shown in the following code:

    ```
    transform.Rotate(rotAxis, rotSpeed * Time.deltaTime);
    ```

7. The `OnTriggerEnter()` method will be invoked whenever the collider of this object collides with another collider in the world; incidentally, if we set `IsTrigger=false` on our `gameObject`, the `OnCollisionEnter()` method will be dispatched instead of `OnTriggerEnter()`. Note, for Unity to dispatch either of these callbacks, we must remember to add a **Rigidbody** component to the GameObject of `InteractiveObj` at the design time in the editor.

8. Note, when Unity dispatches this callback, it passes in another parameter of the `collider` type. This collider is the collider of the object that entered the trigger volume. Convenient! The signature looks as follows:

    ```
    OnTriggerEnter(other collider)
    {
    }
    ```

9. In this method, we check that the other object (the `gameObject` that has just entered this collider) has a tag equal to `Player`, as shown in the next line of code. This is how we ensure that our trigger only responds to entities that we specify (we must remember to set the tag on the player `gameObject` to `Player`):

    ```
    if (other.gameObject.tag == "Player")
    ```

10. If the `OnCloseEnough` object interaction is not null, we dereference it and invoke the `handleInteraction()` method. In our example, this method does the work of inserting objects into the inventory as shown in the following code:

```
if (OnCloseEnough != null)
{
    OnCloseEnough.handleInteraction();
}
```

Congratulations! We now have a class that implements an interactive object. Let's continue further with an `ObjectInteraction` script that this class can utilize.

Implementing the ObjectInteraction script

The `ObjectInteraction` class defines how the interactive object will be manipulated when an interaction occurs between the object and the player. Perform the following steps to implement this:

1. Two enumerations are required to specify the action and the type of action. The action will be what we do with the item (put in inventory and use) initially, as shown in the following code:

```
public enum InteractionAction
{
    Invalid = -1,
    PutInInventory = 0,
    Use = 1,
}
```

2. The corresponding type specializes this behavior by determining if the object is unique or can be accumulated with other interactive objects of the similar type. A unique interaction specifies that `ObjectIneraction` will insert this interactive object in a unique slot in `InventoryMgr`, while an accumulate interaction specifies that `ObjectInteraction` will insert this item (and increase the quantity) in the first available slot that matches the type set in `CustomGameObj`, as shown in the following code:

```
public enum InteractionType
{
    Invalid = -1,
    Unique = 0,
    Accumulate = 1,
}
```

3. We keep the following two public variables to store the two enumerations discussed in the previous step:

```
public InteractionAction interaction;
public InteractionType interactionType;
```

4. We also keep a `Texture` variable to store the icon that will be displayed in the inventory for this GameObject as follows:

```
public Texture tex;
```

5. The `HandleInteraction()` method of this class works on the interactive object that this script is attached to. To begin, we get the `InventoryMgr` component off the player if it can be found. Don't worry that we haven't created the `InventoryMgr` yet; we will!

```
if (player)
   iMgr = player.GetComponent<InventoryMgr>();
```

6. As we extend the number of interaction types that our game supports, this method will grow. For now, if `PutInInventory` is the type, we will delegate `i=InventoryMgr` to add this `InteractiveObj` to its collection as follows:

```
if (interaction == InteractionAction.PutInInventory)
{
   if (iMgr)
      iMgr.Add(this.gameObject.GetComponent<interactiveObj ();
}
```

Congratulations! You have implemented an `ObjectInteraction` class that operates on the `InteractiveObj` class. Let's continue by implementing the `InventoryItem` class.

Implementing the InventoryItem script

The `InventoryItem` class is the base item container that the `InventoryMgr` collection is built from. It contains a reference to `GameObject` that has been inserted in the inventory (via the `ObjectInteraction` class). It also has a copy of the texture to display in the inventory as well as the number of objects that a particular `InventoryItem` represents, as shown in the following code:

```
public Texture displayTexture;
public GameObject item;
public int quantity;
```

Scripts that inherit from `monobehavior` can be fully manipulated by the Unity3D Editor; they can be attached to GameObjects, have the property values saved, among other things. This class does not inherit from `monobehavior`; as it is an internal helper class for `InventoryMgr`. It never has to be attached to GameObject (a programmer or designer would not normally want to attach one of these to a 3D object because it doesn't need a `Transform` component to do its work). This class only acts as the glue between the interactive objects that have been collected and the UI button that `InventoryMgr` displays for these objects' custom type. Hence, this class does not derive from any base class. This allows us to declare a list of these objects directly inside `InventoryMgr`.

To make the class show up in the inspector (in `InventoryMgr`), we need to add back some of the functionality that would have been included, had we inherited from `monobehavior`; namely, the serialization of its properties. Hence, we add the following code decoration before the class declaration:

```
[System.Serializable]
```

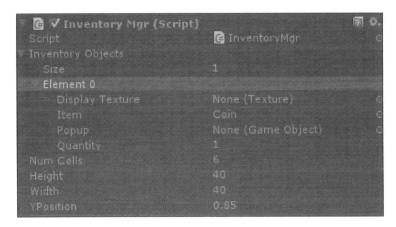

Implementing the InventoryMgr script

The `InventoryMgr` class contains the system that manages the `InteractiveObj` classes that the player collects. It displays inventory items in an inventory panel at the bottom of the screen. It has a method for adding inventory items and displaying inventory at the bottom of the screen. Perform the following steps to implement the `InventoryMgr` script:

1. To begin, recall that the class declaration for this system follows the same pattern as the others that were created with the new script wizard. Until this point, however, we haven't included any other namespaces than the default two: `UnityEngine` and `System.Collections`. For this class, note that we add using `System.Collections.Generic` in the code. Doing this gives us access to the `List<>` datatype in our scripts, which we will need to store the collection of inventory objects, as shown in the following code:

```
using UnityEngine;
using System.Collections;
using System.Collections.Generic;

public class InventoryMgr : MonoBehaviour {

public List<InventoryItem> inventoryObjects = new
List<InventoryItem>();
```

2. The `InventoryMgr` class also has parameters that describe the way in which the constraints on the UI will be displayed, along with a reference to the `MissionMgr` script, as shown in the following code:

```
public int numCells;
public float height;
public float width;
public float yPosition;
private MissionMgr missionMgr;
```

3. In the `Start()` method, when this class is first created, we will find the object in the scene named **Game**, and store a reference to the `MissionMgr` script that is attached to it, as shown in the following code:

```
void Start () {
  GameObject go = GameObject.Find ("Game");
  if (go)
    missionMgr = go.GetComponent<MissionMgr>();
}
```

4. The `Add()` method is used by `ObjectInteraction.handleInteraction()` to insert an `InteractiveObj` in the inventory (when it is picked up). Recall that the signature looks as follows:

```
public void Add(InteractiveObj iObj)
{
    ObjectInteraction oi = iObj.OnCloseEnough;
```

5. Based on the `ObjectInteraction` type specified in the interaction, the `Add()` method will behave in specialized ways, and a `switch` statement is used to select which specific behavior to use. If the `ObjectInteraction` type is `Unique`, then `InventoryMgr` inserts this `InteractiveObj` in the first available slot, as shown in the following code:

```
switch(oi.interactionType)
{
    case(ObjectInteraction.interactionType.Unique):
    {
        // slot into first available spot
        Insert(iObj);
    }
    break;
```

6. If the `ObjectInteraction` type is `Accumulate`, then `InventoryMgr` will insert this in the first slot that matches the `CustomGameObject` type on the interactive object. To determine this matching, we first store a reference to the `CustomGameObject` script on the interactive object that is being inserted. If this object does not have a `CustomGameObject` script, we assume the type is `Invalid`, as shown in the following code:

```
case(ObjectInteraction.InteractionType.Accumulate):
{
    bool inserted = false;

    // find object of same type, and increase
    CustomGameObject cgo = iObj.gameObject.GetComponent
    <CustomGameObject>();

    CustomGameObject.CustomObjectType ot = CustomGameObject.
    CustomObjectType.Invalid;

    if (cgo != null)
        ot = cgo.objectType;
```

7. The `InventoryMgr` class then loops over all inventory objects in the list. If it finds an object that has a matching `CustomGameObject` type to the interactive object that is being inserted, it increases the quantity property on that `InventoryObj`. If a match is not found, then `InventoryObj` is permitted to be inserted in the list as if it were a unique item, as shown in the following code:

```
for (int i = 0; i < inventoryObjects.Count; i++)
{
CustomGameObject cgoi = inventoryObjects[i].item.GetComponent
<CustomGameObject>();
CustomGameObject.CustomObjectType io = CustomGameObject.
CustomObjectType.Invalid;
    if (cgoi != null)
      io = cgoi.objectType;

    if (ot == io)
    {
      inventoryObjects[i].quantity++;
      // add token from this object to missionMgr
      // to track, if this obj as a token
      MissionToken mt = iObj.gameObject.GetComponent<MissionToken>();

      if (mt != null)
        missionMgr.Add(mt);

      iObj.gameObject.SetActive(false);
      inserted = true;
      break;
    }
}
```

8. Note, if the types of the object match any existing object on the list, we do some book keeping. We increase its number as well as copy the texture reference that we will display in the inventory. We will also disable the object (to stop it from rendering and interacting with the world) by setting its active flag to `false` and then we leave the loop, as shown in the following code. We will declare the `MissionToken` script later in this chapter:

```
    if (ot == io)
    {
      inventoryObjects[i].quantity++;
missionTokenmt = iObj.gameObject.GetComponent<MissionToken>();
iObj.gameObject.SetActive (false);
      inserted = true;
    }
```

9. An important aspect to note here is that we need to check if there is a
    `MissionToken` script attached to this `InteractiveObj`. If there is one,
    then we will add it to `MissionMgr`. In this way, we will complete the
    communication between the two management systems in this chapter.
    Later, we will see how `MissionMgr` searches for complete missions and
    rewards the player using mechanics similar to those discussed earlier:

    ```
    if (mt != null)
       missionMgr.Add(mt);
    ```

10. The `Insert()` method of `InventoryMgr` is used to perform the actual
    insertion work in the list of inventory objects. It is declared with the
    following signature:

    ```
    void Insert(InteractiveObj iObj){
    }
    ```

11. This method first allocates a new `InventoryItem` with the `new` operator.
    We have to use `new` instead of `Object.Instantiate` to create a new instance
    of this class because this class does not inherit from `Object`. With a new
    instance of `InventoryItem` available for use, we will populate its properties
    with the data from `InteractiveObj`, as shown in the following code:

    ```
    InventoryItem ii = new InventoryItem();
       ii.item = iObj.gameObject;
       ii.quantity = 1;
    ```

12. Then, we will disable GameObject of `InteractiveObj` (just in case it is still
    enabled), and finally add the `InventoryItem` to the list with a direct call to
    `inventoryObjects.add`, as shown in the following code:

    ```
    ii.item.SetActive (false);
    inventoryObjects.Add (ii);
    ```

13. Lastly, just in case there is `MissionToken` attached to this GameObject from
    some other code path, we will extract the token and add it to `MissionMgr` for
    tracking, as shown in the following code:

    ```
    MissionToken mt = ii.item.GetComponent<MissionToken>();
    if (mt != null)
       missionMgr.Add(mt);
    ```

And this completes the work on the `Insert()` method.

Implementing the DisplayInventory method

Let's continue our work by developing `InventoryMgr` as we program the method that will display all of the inventory objects on screen by performing the following steps:

1. The `DisplayInventory()` method is declared with the following signature:

    ```
    void DisplayInventory() {
    }
    ```

2. This method also walks through the collection, but instead of checking the type of object, it will display a series of GUI buttons on the screen. It will also show `displayTexture` for the item in each inventory. As the position of the inventory cells are relative to the screen, we need to calculate the button positions based on the screen width and height, as shown in the following code:

    ```
    float sw = Screen.width;
    float sh = Screen.height;
    ```

3. We will also store a reference to the texture we will display in each cell, as shown in the following code:

    ```
    Texture buttonTexture = null;
    ```

4. Then, for clarity, we will store the number of cells in a local integer to display as shown in the following code:

    ```
    int totalCellsToDisplay = inventoryObjects.Count;
    ```

5. We will loop over all the cells and extract the texture and quantity in each `InventoryItem` in the collection, as shown in the following code:

    ```
    for (int i = 0; i<totalCellsToDisplay; i++)
    {
       InventoryItem ii = InventoryObjects[i];
       t = ii.displayTexture;
       int quantity = ii.quantity;
    ```

e result of this code is shown as follows:

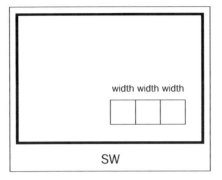

6.   We will compute the total length of all the cells that we want to display. This is used in the code to render the cells centered in the middle of the screen horizontally. Recall that the width and height hold the individual cell width and height:

```
float totalCellLength = sw - (numcells * width);
```

As `InventoryMgr` loops over all `InventoryObjects`, we draw a new rectangle for each item to be displayed on the screen. To do this, we need to know the *x*, *y* coordinates of the upper-left corner of the rectangle, the height and width of an individual rectangle, and the texture. The *y* height doesn't vary since the inventory is a horizontal row on screen, and the cell height and width don't vary since the cells are uniform by design. The texture will change, but we can use the cached value. So, we need to focus our attention on the *x* coordinate for a centered array of varying length.

7.   It turns out that we can use this formula. The `totalCellLength` parameter is the amount of white space horizontally when all the cells are aligned on one side. If we subtract half of this, we get the starting coordinate that will be positioned half on the right and half on the left equally. Considering that width and height are the dimensions of the individual buttons for display and that *i* is the loop index for the loop we are discussing, then adding `(width*i)` ensures that the subsequent *x* coordinates vary horizontally across the array, as shown in the following code:

```
float xcoord = totalCellLength - 0.5f*(totalCellLength)
+(width*i);
```

8. The rectangle that corresponds to the shape of the button we want to display is then calculated with the following formula. Note that its position on the screen is a function of *i*, the loop index, as well as *y*, the screen width and height, and the button width and height:

```
Rect r = new Rect(totalCellLength - 0.5f*(totalCellLength) +
(width*i), yPosition*sh, width, height);
```

With all of these quantities now calculated, we will display the button with the `GUI.button(r, buttonTexture)` method, as shown in the following code. We will check for a `true` return value from this function because this is how we track when the user clicks on a button:

```
if (GUI.Button(r, buttonTexture))
{
  // to do - handle clicks there
}
```

9. Recall that we need to display the number of items with each button. We do this with the `GUI.Label` method in a way analogous to the previous code. We will compute a second rectangle for the quantity that mirrors the cell for the button, but we will use half the cell width and height to position the rectangle in the upper-left corner for a nice effect!

10. We will convert the quantity field of the current `InventoryItem` class to a string with the built-in function called `ToString()` that the integer implements, and we will pass this to the `GUI.Label` method, as shown in the following code:

```
Istring s = quantity.ToString()
GUI.Label(r2, s);
```

11. To display UI textures and elements on the screen, Unity provides a special callback method to place our UI code whenever the UI is refreshed. This method is called `OnGui()` and has the following signature:

```
void OnGUI(){
}
```

12. We invoke our `DisplayInventory()` method inside the `void OnGUI()` method that Unity provides because this method draws the `InventoryItems` list of `InventoryMgr` to the screen in the form of UI buttons. This callback is where all drawing and GUI-related processing occurs, as shown in the following code:

```
void OnGUI()
{
  DisplayInventory();
}
```

We could modify this code slightly to draw the maximum number of cells in the inventory rather than the total number of filled `InventoryMgr` cells. We must be careful to not dereference past the end of the collection if we have been doing so!

Congratulations! We now have a working `InventoryMgr` system that can interface with interactive objects and collect them based on their custom type! While we touched briefly on the `MissionToken` class in this explanation, we need to develop a system for tracking the abstract mission objectives and rewarding the player on achieving success. This requires multiple classes. The result of performing these steps is shown in the following screenshot:

Implementing the MissionMgr script

The `MissionMgr` class tracks the user's progress through abstract objectives. These objectives will be learning objectives that satisfy the game design. The pattern we use to manage missions will be similar to `InventoryMgr`; however, this system will be in charge of comparing the player's objectives with a master list of missions and with what is required to complete each one. To develop it, let's perform the following steps:

1. To accomplish this work, `MissionMgr` will need two lists. One list to hold all of the missions that the player could try and solve and another for the current tokens that the player has acquired (through interacting with interactive objects, for instance). The `MissionTokens` collection is allocated at runtime and set to empty so that the player always starts having accomplished nothing; we could develop a way later to load and save the mission progress via this system. The missions' list will be populated at runtime in the editor and saved, so we don't want to initialize this at runtime:

   ```
   Public List<mission> missions;
   Public List<missionToken> missionTokens = new
   List<missionTokens>();
   ```

2. The `MissionMgr` implements three methods that allow it to perform its role and interface with other game systems:

   ○ `Add(missionToken)`: This method adds a newly acquired `MissionToken` to the collection. This collection will be queried while trying to determine if a mission has been completed. In `Add()`, we use a similar methodology as the `Add()` method for `InventoryMgr`. In this case, assume that the token is unique and search for a duplicate by iterating over all of the tokens for the current mission m, as shown in the following code:

   ```
   bool uniqueToken = true;
   for (int i = 0; i<missionTokens.Count; i++)
   {
     //...
   }
   ```

   If a duplicate is found, namely, a token is found in the collection with the same id field as the add candidate, we abort the operation as shown in the following code:

   ```
   if (missionTokens[i].id == mt.id)
   {
   ```

```
  // duplicate token found, so abort the insert
  uniqueToken = false;
  break;
}
```

If a duplicate is not found, we add this token to the list as shown in the following code:

```
if (uniqueToken)
{
  missionTokens.add(mt);
}
```

° `Validate(mission)`: This method will compare `currentToken` set to a specific mission. If it has been found to have been satisfied, the system is notified. To do this, we will use a search pattern similar to the one used in the `Add()` method and start by assuming the mission is complete; only this time we will use a double-nested loop! This is because to validate a mission means to search, individually, for each token in the current mission against all of the tokens the user has collected so far. This is done as shown in the following code:

```
bool missionComplete = true;
for (intinti = 0; I < m.tokens.Count; i++)
{
  bool tokenFound = false;
  for (int j = 0; j < missionTokens.count ; j++)
  {
    // if tokens match, tokenFound = true
  }
}
```

By assuming the token will not be found initially, we are required to search for a matching token ID. If we don't find it, it automatically means that the mission cannot be complete, and we don't have to process any more comparisons, as shown in the following code:

```
if (tokenFound == true))
{
  missionComplete = false;
  break;
}
```

- ○ ValidateAll(): This methods invokes Validate() on all user-defined missions if they are not already complete. If any mission is found to be completed, a reward is instantiated for the player through the InvokeReward() method, as shown in the following code:

```
void ValidateAll() {

  for (int i = 0; i < missions.Count; i++)
  {
    Mission m = missions[i];

    // validate missions…
  }
}
```

We will sequentially search through all user-defined missions that have not already been completed (no need to do this once a mission is done). This enumeration will be defined in the Mission script, as shown in the following code:

```
if (m.status != mission.missionStatus.MS_Completed)
{
  bool missionSuccess = Validate(m);
```

If the mission has been validated as being complete, the mission implements an InvokeReward() method to reward the user, as shown in the following code:

```
if (missionSuccess == true)
{
  m.InvokeReward();
}
```

Implementing the Mission script

The Mission class is the container for MissionTokens. It implements a state that helps us specialize how a mission should be treated by the game (for instance, we may want to have the player acquire a mission but not start it). This class has a number of state variables for future extension such as activated, visible, and points.

1. As with the `InventoryItem` class, the `Mission` class is a helper class that only the `MissionMgr` class uses. Hence, it does not inherit from `monobehavior`. Therefore, the class signature must include the `[System.Serializable]` tag as before:

```
using UnityEngine;
using System.Collections;
using System.Collections.Generic;

[System.Serializable]
public class Mission {
```

2. This class also implements an enumeration to describe the state of a particular mission. This is used to encode whether a state is invalid, acquired, in progress, or solved so that `MissionMgr` can handle the mission appropriately, as shown in the following code:

```
public enum missionStatus
{
    MS_Invalid = -1,
    MS_Acquired = 0,
    MS_InProgress = 1,
    MS_Completed = 2
};
```

3. The public variable status is an instance variable of the status enumerated type in this class. We will use this initially to make sure that once a mission is complete, `MissionMgr` no longer tries to validate it. This can be done with the following code:

```
Public missionStatus status;
```

4. The specific elements that comprise a mission are the mission tokens that the user puts in the tokens' collection. This is a collection of logical pieces that comprises a complete objective in the game. This list will be compared against the players' acquired tokens in `MissionMgr`, as shown in the following code:

```
Public List<missionTokens> tokens;
```

5. The `points` and `reward` public variables are used to store the numerical score and the in-game rewards that are given to the user when a mission is completed. Note, `GameObject reward` could be used as a completion callback, in addition to a reference to a Prefab item for the user to pick up, as shown in the following code:

```
public int points;
public GameObject reward;
```

6. The `displayName` public variable is used by the user in the Unity3D Editor as a place for a helpful string to describe the mission's nature, as shown in the following code:

```
public string displayName;
```

This class implements one method: the `InvokeReward()` method. This function will spawn a new `gameObject` into the world that has been set in the editor. Through this mechanism, the player can be rewarded with points, a new object or objective can appear in the world, or any other outcome can be encapsulated in a Unity `Prefab` object.

7. Once a mission has been validated and `InvokeReward` has been called, the mission itself is disabled and its status is set to `Completed`, as shown in the following code:

```
this.status = missionStatus.MS_Completed;
```

Implementing the MissionToken script

The `MissionToken` class stores the information for an individual mission component. This class acts as a container for this abstract data. We give it an ID, a title that is human readable, and a description. By giving each `MissionToken` a unique ID, we give the `Mission` class a powerful way of tracking the mission progress. This class is used in a way by which the user adds instances of this component to various interactive objects that can be manipulated by the player, as shown in the following code:

```
Public int id;
Public string title;
Public string description;
```

Implementing the SimpleLifespanScript

The `SimpleLifespanScript` class is a simple helper class that can be used in conjunction with the `Instantiate()` method to instantiate a GameObject in the world that will have a specified but finite lifespan. We use it to enable an instance of a Prefab that is live for a set period of time and then destroys itself as a reward for completing a mission. By attaching this to the reward that is displayed when a mission is completed, the prompt is given a set duration on the screen after which it disappears.

Specifically, the `seconds` parameter is the time for which the object will survive before self destruction, as shown in the following code:

```
Public float seconds
```

In the `update` method, we count this value by the actual time elapsed in each frame (from `Timer.deltaTime`). Once this reaches zero, we destroy the object and all the scripts attached to it (including the `simpleLifespanScript`), as shown in the following code:

```
seconds -= Time.deltaTime;
if (seconds <= 0.0f)
   GameObject.Destroy(this.gameObject);
```

Congratulations! We now have a robust set of scripts for `MissionMgr`, missions, tokens, and rewards. Let's apply what we have built in an example that exercises the mission system, the inventory system, and interactive objects.

Putting it all together

Now that we have developed the classes necessary for the `InventoryMgr`, `MissionMgr`, and `InteractiveObj` systems, let's build a scene that illustrates their functionality.

1. To get started, let's continue from *Chapter 1, Introduction to E-Learning and the Three Cs of 3D Games*, where we left off. Load the scene and save a copy named `chapter2`.

2. Add an instance of `InventoryMgr` to the `Player` GameObject by dragging-and-dropping it from the **Project** tab to the `player` object. Alternatively, click on **Player** and select **Add component** from the **Inspector** pane. Type in the name `InventoryMgr` and then click on it to add an instance.

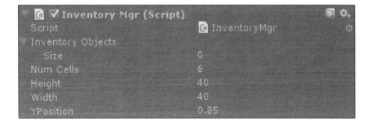

3. Click on **Player** and ensure that the **Tag** is set to **Player**. The `InteractiveObj` class will use this to make sure they can only be picked up by the player.

4. Set **Height** and **Width** to **40** pixels to make the individual cells square shaped. Set the **Yposition** to **0.85** to indicate a *y* coordinate of 85 percent from the top of the screen.

5. Create a new empty GameObject and name it `MissionMgr`. Attach the `MissionMgr` script to this object. We purposely detach this script from the player because the lifespan of `MissionMgr` may differ from the player object.

The results of all the discussed settings are shown in the following screenshot:

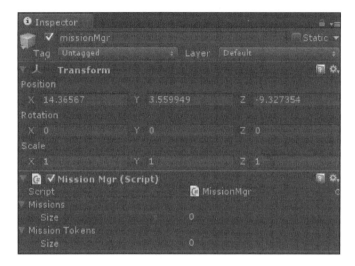

Now that we have added our new tracking systems to the game, let's create some objects to interact with:

1. Create a sphere and place it on the ground plane. Name it `A_Coin` and disable the mesh renderer component. On the sphere collider, click the **IsTrigger** checkbox so that we can detect when the player enters the object.

2. Add a **Rigidbody** component to the object. This is necessary for the `OnTriggerEnter` callback to be dispatched by the engine. Remember, the way Unity detects when the player (or any other object) enters a trigger is by checking its **Rigidbody** component; so, if there is no such component attached, the the callback will not be dispatched.

3. Add a `CustomGameObject` script to this object. Set the display name to `money` and the object type to `coin`.

4. Add a `MissionToken` script to this object. Set **id** to `1`, **Title** to `token`, and the **Description** to `mission 1 token`.

5. Add an `InteractiveObj` script to this object. Set **Rot Axis** to (0, 1, 0) to make the object rotate horizontally about the *y* axis. Set **Rot Speed** to 40 for a gentle rotation.

6. Add an `ObjectInteraction` script to this object. Set the interaction to `putInInventory`. Set the interaction type to `accumulate`. Point `Tex` to the `Coin-icon` coin texture.

7. Drag-and-drop this `gameObject` into the `OnCloseEnough` variable of the `InteractiveObject` component. This will connect this reference to the `ObjectInteraction` component on `gameObject` itself.

8. Now that the script is wired up, let's add a yellow coin model to the coin base. Create a cylinder `gameObject`, parent it to the `A_Coin` base, and set its local position to (0, 0, 0). Create a material, colored yellow, and attach it to the mesh renderer of the cylinder.

9. Set its rotation to (90, 0, 0) in the inspector. Set its scale to (0, 0.16, 0) in the inspector as well.

    The result of all these steps can be seen in the following screenshot:

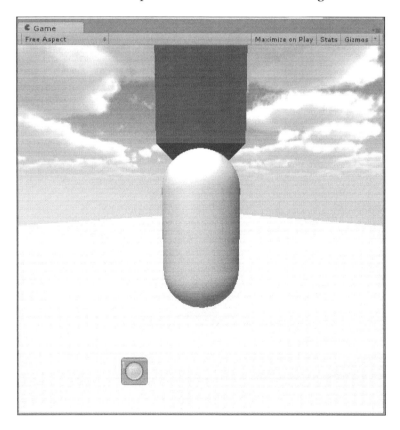

Congratulations! We now have one interactive object in the world. To test this, let's click on play and observe a slowly rotating coin. If we then walk the player up to it so that he or she can collect it, we will then see the inventory displaying the item.

Testing the mission system

Let's add another type of interactive object and then build a couple of missions to finish validating our work.

1. Drag-and-drop this A_Coin object from the **Hierarchy** tab into the **Project** tab, thereby creating a Prefab. Name this Prefab coin, as shown in the following screenshot:

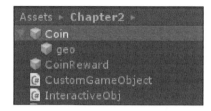

2. Create a second interactive object, following the steps 1 to 9 from the *Building an interactive object* section. Instead of making a yellow coin, create a red ruby and point the inventory texture to the ruby icon texture provided.

3. Name this object A_Ruby and set the mission token ID to 4.

4. Drag-and-drop A_Ruby to the **Project** tab, forming a Prefab named Ruby.

5. Drag-and-drop the coin and ruby Prefabs back into the **Hierarchy** tab. At this point, there should be two coins and two rubies. Set the mission token ID of the second coin to 2 and the second ruby to 4.

Now that we have two coins and two rubies, let's create two missions!

1. Click on MissionMgr and increase the size of the missions' array to 2. Note that the array populates with an empty version of the Mission class. Set the first mission to activated and visible.

2. Set the first mission state to **MS_ACQUIRED** and name it **Coin Craze**.

3. Set the description to **collect all of the coins**.

4. Set the points to **500**.

5. Under tokens, drag-and-drop the two coin game objects. This will set the references to MissionTokens attached to the coin Prefabs.

6. Create a reward Prefab out of `GuiText` with `SimpleLifeSpanScript` attached. Set the string to **You have completed the coin challenge** with a lifespan of 2 seconds. Drag-and-drop this Prefab into the reward field of `mission 1` in the mission manager. Make sure to delete any instances of this reward Prefab from the hierarchy; we want `MissionMgr` to spawn this!

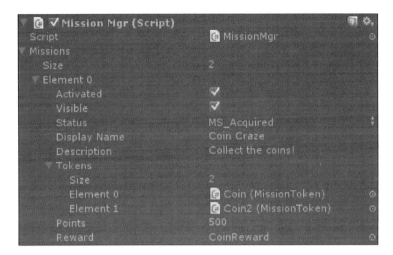

7. Follow steps 7 to 12 from the *Building an interactive object* section again, only this time name the mission **Ruby Run** and point the mission tokens to the two ruby instances in the world (with unique mission token IDs). Create a new reward for this mission and drag-and-drop its Prefab onto the reward for mission 2.

8. Position the coins and rubies in the world at random locations in the game world. Play the level to observe `MissionMgr` in action, as shown in the following screenshot:

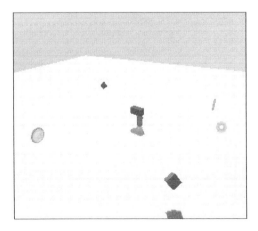

Try it out!

Congratulations! We now have two missions with which we can test interactive objects and player mission objectives. Note that when you play the game, you can collect the items in any order and that the inventory will update the quantity of objects from one to two as you collect them. The reward displays for two seconds and then the mission disables itself.

Summary

We have learned how to develop interactive objects, an inventory system, and a mission tracking system. We have shown examples of how components attached to GameObject can communicate with one another. We have extensively used the list container and the search pattern to implement tracking and inventory maintenance methods. Going forward, we will use these systems in conjunction with a little applied psychology and gamification theory to develop the first mission in our game.

Mission One – Find the Facts

3

Recall that in the first two chapters, we developed the core technology for a camera, player controls, interactive objects, and a mission-tracking system. Now it's time to apply our technology and make our first learning objective. Our e-learning game will educate the user on the 50 American states, the state flags, and some state trivia. In this chapter, we will assemble the systems we have created thus far and develop our first playable game level—the first of three in our final game.

In this chapter, we will cover the following topics:

- Introducing mission one: find the facts
- Designing games to maximize fun
- Implementing the core classes for mission one
- Playing the level

Finding the facts

In this game, the hero (player) plays the park ranger in charge of cleaning up Confederation National Park. In mission one, the park ranger has to find the missing flags for the flag monument and return them to their holders. The user will have to find five of 50 US flags. They will be placed at random locations in the world. The user will have to collect them, read about the associated states' trivia, and then bring the flags back once all the five flags have been found. The game comprises the following components:

- `FlagLocators`: This `GameObject` hierarchy contains a set of potential flag locations. From these 10 potential locations, five will be randomly chosen.

- `Terrain`: We introduce the terrain editor in this chapter and create a terrain mesh to replace the ground plane from *Chapter 2, Interactive Objects and MissionMgr*. As our design requires us to have a park-like setting for our game, the terrain editor is the best candidate for building this in the editor quickly and easily; the alternative is modelling the park in a 3D modelling program such as Maya and then exporting and importing into Unity. By adding grass, mountains, and trees we create a picturesque park that will serve as the backdrop and scene for our first game environment.

- `Monument`: This GameObject hierarchy contains a set of five flagmount locations. These are the places where the flags will be attached once the user finds the missing flags and returns them.

- `MissionMgrHelper`: This helper class allows a GameObject to manipulate the state of an already-existing mission. This is done by associating the script with a Prefab and then instantiating after a user interaction.

- `SetupMissionOne`: To accomplish the objectives of the level, this class installs two missions in the `MissionMgr` class that we developed in the previous chapter and also picks the random flags and flag locations for those missions.

- `TriviaCardScript`: This class displays a full screen texture on screen that represents a trivia card for a state. The script adjusts the size and layout of the texture and displays it centered on screen. These cards will appear when the flags are first picked up and when they are selected in the inventory.

- `MonumentMgr`: The gameplay objective of this level is to locate flags and return them to a monument with a number of empty mounting points. This class provides an interface for the monument hierarchy to attach an object (a returned flag) to one of the monument's flagmount points.

- `SimpleDetachScript`: This class detaches the GameObject that it is attached to, from any parent transforms, thereby making its parent the global coordinates. This is necessary for packaging `GUITextures` in a Prefab for instancing and then previewing.

The first two collections will be referenced by `SetupMissionOne`, which picks the flag locations, picks five Prefabs, and instances them. A number of Prefabs will need to be created as well to facilitate the flow logic across missions. Finally, some systems from *Chapter 1, Introduction to E-Learning and the Three Cs of 3D Games*, and *Chapter 2, Interactive Objects and MissionMgr*, will be updated to improve the gameplay.

Designing games to maximize fun

Prior to designing the first playable level in the game, an understanding of how to model fun in games is required. Have you ever been involved in an activity and lost track of time, such as playing a game or otherwise? Cognitive psychologists call this mental state *flow*, and it is thought to be one way of maximizing fun. This is desirable because when the user is most engaged and having fun, learning and retention of information is maximized.

Game designers are interested in how we can design games that maximize the likelihood of the user entering this mental state.

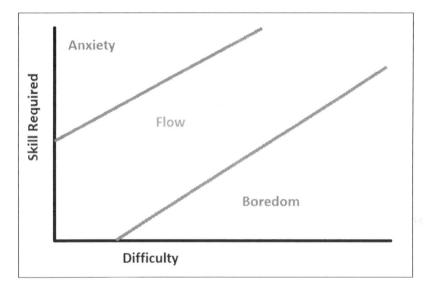

It turns out that we have a model for how to entice the user to achieve flow. Consider the previous diagram that illustrates the relationship between the difficulty and the skill required for a given task. This is when the activity is moderately challenging and under moderate pressure. If the activity is too hard or too easy, or if the situation is too boring or too stressful, it reduces the likelihood of maximizing fun via the flow model.

The teaching loop in game design

There are three stages of teaching in games described as follows:

- **Presentation**: In this stage, factual information is presented to the user. In a gaming situation, the user participates in engaging game mechanics to discover or interact with the objective material to be learned. The game mechanics provide incentives and challenges to encourage the player to enter flow.

- **Application**: In this stage, the user participates in game mechanics while employing the facts from stage one. The game mechanics reinforce good behavior as well as recall and mastery of the material from stage one. The game also reduces negative behavior—failure to recall and master the material from stage one.

- **Synthesis**: In this stage, through interactions with novel game scenarios, the user has to apply the mastered knowledge to new situations. By doing this, mastery and consolidation is further heightened, and a higher level understanding and insight is achieved in the subject matter.

Implementing the core classes for mission one

In this chapter, we will start creating mission one, which presents US geography to the player (state name, flag, and trivia). Let's begin by creating the classes and `GameObject` instances for this level. To begin, create a new scene file and name it `TESTBED`.

Creating a terrain

Let's create a nice terrain mesh to replace the ground plane from the previous two levels. With this, we can create a nice-looking mesh for the ground that resembles a park with grass, mountains, and trees by performing the following steps:

1. In the **Assets** menu, navigate to **Import Package | Terrain Assets**. Click on the **Import** button on the pop-up window that appears next to bring a library of models and textures into Unity for use with the terrain editor.

2. To create a terrain mesh, let's navigate to **CreateOther | Terrain**, from the **GameObject** drop-down list.

3. On the **Set Heightmap resolution** pop up that appears, configure the parameters to the following values:

- ° **Terrain Width, Terrain Length**: The horizontal dimensions of the terrain mesh. Set both to 500 units.

- ° **Terrain Height**: The maximum height of the terrain (for mountains and so on). Set this to 500 units.

- ° The remaining parameters control the resolution of the textures that are painted onto the terrain. Keep these at their defaults.

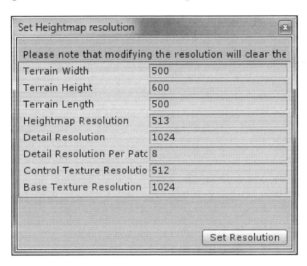

4. Click on the new terrain GameObject in the **Hierarchy** view, set its position to -250, 0, -250. This will place the terrain in the 3D world at a convenient location that results in the middle of the terrain at the world origin, which is convenient for development.

5. Clicking on the new terrain, observe the seven unique radio buttons on the terrain component in the inspector tab as shown in the following screenshot:

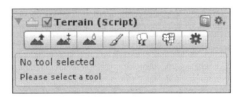

6. The first one from left-hand side will raise or lower terrain depending on if *Shift* or *Ctrl* are held down while clicking and moving the mouse. Zoom out in the scene view; select one of the many interesting brushes; and try creating some mountains. Note the effect that brush size and opacity has on the deformations to the terrain.

7. The second button allows you to paint to a certain height. This is good for fine control of elevation in a terrain mesh if you want to build very specific configurations of plateaus.

8. The third button is the smooth height button. Use this if you have previously painted some elevations with a brush that has lots of bumps and jagged edges. This brush will average and round out the selected peaks.

9. The fourth button is the paint textures button. If you navigate to **Edit Textures | Add Texture**, you can select a texture from any of the imported textures in the project thus far. Click on the texture viewer panel (rather than the normal map panel) to see a dialog box of all available options. After selecting and confirming, you will see your selection as an option back in the terrain previewer. Now, with your favorite brush selected, you can paint the texture onto your terrain. Add a variety of textures to paint grass, roads, and mountain details into your terrain.

10. The next button lets you paint tree models into your scene. Select a tree model from the edit trees button, and once you have confirmed a selection, choose a brush and density to paint the models with. A low-density circle can be used to add foliage to the tops of your mountain ranges. If you find that your game suddenly runs slowly after painting trees, it likely means you have too many tree models on screen. The fix for this is to reduce the density of the trees.

11. The second from the right-hand side button lets you paint the details into your scene. The workflow is similar to painting trees, and they behave similarly as well although this is intended for small details such as grass.

12. The right-most button lets you control the parameters of your terrain component. Things such as wind-speed, draw distances, and grass color let you fine-tune the look of your park.

Once you have finished making your park, it should look somewhat like the following screenshot:

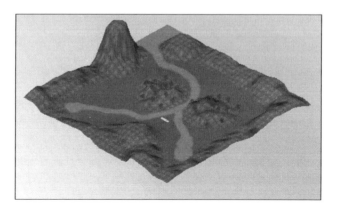

Creating the FlagLocators GameObject

Let's create the hierarchy for `FlagLocators` in the scene as follows:

1. Create 10 **Cube** GameObjects. Place them in a variety of interesting places, well spaced out in the level. Put some of them on the ground, some in the hills, some on the mountains, and so on. Name these `FlagLocator1` to `FlagLocator10`.

2. Disable all of the mesh renderers to make these objects invisible in the rendered scene. We will leave these components attached for debugging, but we don't want to draw them normally. Should we want to see where these locators are later on, we just need to enable the renderers to show the geometry.

3. Create another empty `GameObject`, and name it `FlagLocators`. Drag-and-drop all of the locators from step one underneath this object.

Congratulations! We now have a data collection of potential places for flags to spawn in mission one. We will select five of these in the `SetupMissionOne` script discussed in the following section.

Creating the FlagMonument GameObject

Let's build the geometric structure that will be the focal point of the first mission— the monument that needs the flags returned by performing the following steps:

1. Create a new **Cube** GameObject. Scale it so that it is a long and narrow rectangle on the ground in a central place. Name this monument.

2. Create five short **Cylinder** GameObjects. Name them `FlagMount1` to `FlagMount5`, and parent them to the monument so that they are on top of the monument.

3. This should look very similar to the `FlagLocators` in the **Hierarchy** pane seen previously, but we will also create a `MonumentMgr` class and extend its functionality.

Creating the MonumentMgr Script

This script provides the API for the inventory to attach items to the flag mounts at the conclusion of the level.

The `InventoryMgr` script that we will write in this chapter, will use the methods provided in the `MonumentMgr` script to do this work by performing the following steps:

1. Create a new script, and name it `MonumentMgr.cs`. Attach an instance of it to the monument `GameObject`.

2. Inside the script, add `public List<GameObject>` to store the mount points as shown in the following code. Don't forget to add `using System.Collections.Generic` to the top of the file so that we can declare list properties. Failure to add this line of code will result in compile time errors in your script:

    ```
    public List<GameObject> mountPoints;
    ```

3. Drag-and-drop the individual flag mount points from the monument to this list.

4. We add an `attachObjToMountPoint(GameObject obj, int index)` public method as shown in the following code. We first create an instance or clone of the object passed in, attach the object to the given `mountpoint`, and then zero its local translation and rotation. Doing this forces the object to have the same position and angle as `mountpoint` it is attached to, specifically a zero position and rotation offset relative to `mountpoint`. But remember, order is the key here!

    ```
    public void attachObjToMountPoint(GameObject go, int index)
    {
      GameObject newGo = (GameObject)Instantiate (go,
        mountPoints[index].transform.position,
        mountPoints[index].transform.rotation);
      newGo.SetActive(true);
      newGo.transform.parent = mountPoints[index].transform;
      newGo.transform.localPosition = Vector3.zero;
      newGo.transform.localEulerAngles =
        Vector3.zero;//mount.transform.eulerAngles;
    }
    ```

Congratulations! The monument system is now complete. We will interface with this script in a later mission logic.

Creating the InventoryPlaceOnMonument class

This class loops over all the flags in the inventory and places them on the monument. It loops over all the items and then attaches each one to each successive mount point. This can be created by performing the following steps:

1. Create a new `InventoryPlaceOnMonument.cs` script. This will be attached to a new Prefab for instancing later.

2. This script will cache a copy of the inventory manager by finding the `GameObject` named `Player` and then by getting and storing a reference to the `inventoryMgr` component.

3. This script also caches a copy of monument so that it can interface with the `monumentMgr` class defined previously.

4. In the update loop, this script will take an object from the inventory of index `objectIndex`, remove it from the inventory, and set it to active so that it will render again as shown in the following code:

```
GameObject go =
  inventoryMgr.inventoryObjects[objectIndex].item;
go.SetActive (true);
```

5. If there is a cached monument object in the scene, it will then call `attachObjToMountPoint` and attach this `inventoryObject` to the flag mount using the following code:

```
_monument.GetComponent<MonumentMgr>().attachObjToMountPoint
  (go, objectIndex);
```

Congratulations! You now have written the system that will be used to move the flags from the inventory to the monument at the end of the mission. This script will be attached to a Prefab that we will instance once the second mission is complete.

Creating the MissionMgrHelper script

This script searches through the mission manager and finds a mission by name. Once it finds it, it updates the visible and enabled flags on the mission. This is used to activate the second half of level one's objectives once the first half of the objectives are completed. This script can be created as shown in the following code:

```
using UnityEngine;
using System.Collections;

public class missionMgrHelper : MonoBehaviour {
```

```
public string MissionName;
public bool setActivated;
public bool setVisible;
private MissionMgr _missionMgr;

// Use this for initialization
void Start () {

    _missionMgr = GameObject.Find("Game").GetComponent<MissionMgr>();
}

// Update is called once per frame
void Update () {

    for ( int i = 0 ; i < _missionMgr.missions.Count; i++)
    {
      Mission    m = _missionMgr.missions[i];
      if (m.displayName == MissionName)
      {
        m.activated = setActivated;
        m.visible = setVisible;
      }
    }
}

}
```

Creating the TriviaCardScript script

This helper script will be attached to all GUITexture pop ups used in this level, the flaginfo cards, and the user pop ups that happen when the mission's complete. It centers a texture on screen and scales it to the given dimensions.

1. To draw the texture centered on the screen, we start by calculating the center of the screen, and then we offset by half the size of the texture. The reason we do that is because we draw the texture relative to the upper-left corner.

2. The middle of the screen is assigned using the following code:

    ```
    (ScreenWidth/2.0f, ScreenHeight/2.0f)
    ```

3. The upper-left corner of the texture, relative to the center of the screen, is assigned using the following code:

    ```
    (((ScreenWidth/2.0f) - (textureWidth/2)),
      ((ScreenHeight/2.0f) - (textureHeight/2.0f)))
    ```

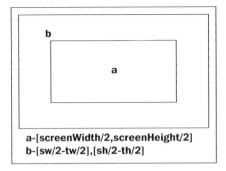

Creating the SetupMissionOne script

This class is used on level startup to configure the world with a random selection of flags for gameplay. This class picks five flags at random and five locations at random. It instances those five flags at those random locations. It also configures the two missions that this level will use to achieve the first learning objective. It is created by performing the following steps:

1. This script will require six individual lists to accomplish its task. Three of them for picking five flags from 50 potential options and three for picking five locations from a set of 10 options.

2. `flagPrefabs` holds all 50 flag Prefabs. This is populated once at design time in the editor as shown in the following code:

   ```
   public List<GameObject> flagPrefabs;
   ```

3. `flagPrefabsBackup` is a copy of the previous list. This occurs once when the game is run. The backup will be used to restore the `flagPrefabs` list if the mission is restarted as shown in the following code:

   ```
   private List<GameObject> flagPrefabsBackup;
   ```

4. `FlagInstances` is the list of five unique, selected `flagPrefabs`. This list is populated from the `flagPrefab` list by choosing an index at random, removing the `GameObject` in the list `flagPrefabs` at that slot, and adding it to the `flagInstances` list as shown in the following code:

   ```
   public List<GameObject> flagInstances;
   ```

5. `spawnPoints` is a list that holds the 10 potential spawn locations for flags in this level as shown in the following code:

   ```
   public List<GameObject> spawnPoints;
   ```

6. spawnPointsBackup is a copy of the previous list. This occurs once when the game is run. The backup will be used to restore the spawnPoints list if the mission is restarted as shown in the following code:

    ```
    public List<GameObject> spawnPointsBackup;
    ```

7. activeSpawnPoints is the list of five unique, selected SpawnPoints. This list is populated from the spawnpoints list by choosing an index at random, removing the GameObject in the SpawnPoints list, slow, and adding it to the activeSpawnPoints list as shown in the following code:

    ```
    public List<GameObject> activeSpawnPoints;
    ```

8. Once the lists of selected spawnpoints and flagprefabs are filled, the script initializes two missions.

9. The first one to be acquired is set to visible and active as shown in the following code:

    ```
    Mission m = missionManager.missions[0];
    m.activated = true;
    m.visible = true;
    m.status = mission.missionStatus.MS_Acquired;
    ```

10. It is also given a displayName and description as shown in the following code:

    ```
    m.displayName = "MissionOne";
    m.description = "collect the 5 randomly placed flags";
    ```

11. For this mission, we instance the five selected flags, place them at the selected spawnpoint, and add them to the MissionMgr. Then we add the five MissionToken script instances (one from each flag Prefab instance) to the mission. This associates picking up each flag instance with the objectives of the first mission as shown in the following code:

    ```
    Vector3 flagPos = activeSpawnPoints[k].transform.position;
    GameObject flagInstance = (GameObject)Instantiate
      (flagPrefab, flagPos, new Quaternion(0.0f, 0.0f, 0.0f,
      1.0f));
    m.tokens.Add (flagInstance.GetComponent<missionToken>());
    ```

12. The second mission is set acquired, visible, and active as shown in the following code:

    ```
    m.activated = false;
    m.visible = false;
    m.status = mission.missionStatus.MS_Acquired;
    ```

13. It is also given a `displayName` and `description` as shown in the following code:

```
m.displayName = "MissionTwo";
m.description = "return the flags to the flagstand";
```

14. All of the `MissionTokens` from mission one are added to mission two as well. Since mission two starts with one `MissionToken` (id=10) in the inspector, the total number of tokens for mission two is equal to six. This last token corresponds to the user taking the five flags back to the monument (the monument gives the user this final flag to complete the mission) as shown in the following code:

```
m.tokens.AddRange (missionManager.missions[0].tokens);
```

Creating the flag Prefabs

As this mission revolves around finding state flags, let's build a generic Prefab that we can texture with different flag imagery, creating a database of objects to choose from.

1. To get started, let's create a cylinder and set it's scale to (0.5, 3.2, 0.5). Create a dark-grey material, and apply it to the cylinder and name it `Pole`.

2. Create a sphere, scale it to (1.5, 0.2, 1.5). Place it on top of the pole and parent it to the cylinder object. Create a yellow material and apply it to the texture as seen in the following screenshot:

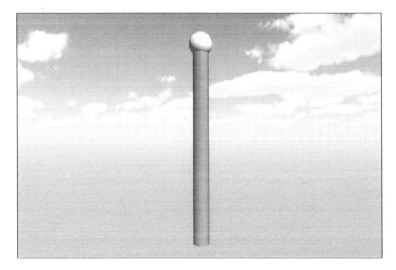

3. Create an interactive cloth object, and orient it by 270 degrees on the *x* axis. Scale it to (1, 0.3, 0.08). Parent it to the pole, and set its local position to (5.8, 0.4, 0). This is a GameObject with script attached that simulates the natural motion of cloth under the influence of external forces. We will use this to build nice-looking flags for the states that respond to gravity, wind, and the player's interactions.

4. Create two more spheres, scaled down to (0.4, 0.07, 0.4). Position these on the pole to act as mount points for the interactive cloth. The cloth will attach at these points to the pole. Disable their mesh renderer so that you cannot see them once they are placed correctly (overlapping the interactive cloth). Make sure that these two spheres have a rigid body component so that they can anchor the interactive cloth properly.

5. Create a new, empty **GameObject**, and name it MissionMgr. Attach the MissionMgr script to this object. We purposely detach this script from the player because the lifespan of MissionMgr may differ from the player object.

Now that we have added our flag geometry, let's create some interactive objects to collect and interact with. As there are 50 states, let's start with Alabama and repeat the following steps for every other state, modifying the textures and state names as appropriate:

1. Create a sphere and place it on the ground plane. Name it Flagpole_ Alabama, and disable the mesh renderer component. On the sphere collider, check the **IsTrigger** checkbox so that we can detect when the player enters the object.

2. Add a CustomGameObject script to this object. Set the display name to Alabama and the object type to flag.

3. Add a mission token script to this object. Set `id=501`, title to `token`, and the description to `mission 1 token`.

4. Add an `InteractiveObj` script to this object. Set the **rotAxis** to (`0,1,0`) to make the object rotate horizontally about the *y* axis. Set the **rot Speed** to `40` for a gentle rotation.

5. Add an object interaction script to this object. Set the interaction to `putInInventory`. Set the interaction type to `Unique`. Point the text to the Alabama state flag texture.

6. Drag-and-drop this `GameObject` into the `OnCloseEnough` variable of the `InteractiveObject` component. This will connect this reference to the `ObjectInteraction` component on the `GameObject` itself.

7. Add an external force of (`1.7,0,0`) and a random force of (`2,2,2`) to the interactive cloth to make the flag flap in the breeze. Consider experimenting with the external force and random force properties of the `InteractiveCloth` script to explore the various different flag behaviors that can be achieved.

We now have a Prefab that we can customize for each state flag. Note the nice animation on the flag when the player walks by it. Let's create 50 Prefabs by applying the correct texture to the interactive cloth component and then dragging the hierarchy into the project tab. Let's also add the following script instances to each Prefab.

1. `CustomGameObject`: Set the object type to `flag`, name it according to the state, and add a reference to the info card for this flag; the info card will show up when the inventory is clicked on, telling the user about the flag, the state name, and some trivia.

2. Add an `InteractiveObj` script, leaving everything as zero except for the reference to `ObjectInteraction` (also an instance on the `flag` Prefab).

3. Add an `ObjectInteraction` script to this object, and connect the reference to the `InteractiveObj` script. Set its parameters to `PutInInventory` and `Unique`, and set the texture to the state flag texture; the text will be the icon that shows up in the inventory when this item is collected.

4. Add a `MissionToken` script. Name the token the same as the state, and give each flag a unique ID ranging from 0 to 50.

Congratulations! Once you have done this 50 times (it may take a while), you will have 50 state flag Prefabs. These should then be added to the `flagPrefabs` list in the `SetupMissionOne` script.

Creating the pop-up card Prefabs

This game level communicates the learning objectives to the player through the information cards. This information will be baked onto a single texture in your favorite external pixel art program. When the player picks up a flag, or presses on the flag button in the inventory, a pop-up card for the relevant state is displayed as shown in the following screenshot:

The pop-up card Prefabs can be created by performing the following steps:

1. Create a new `GUITexture` object, and name it `popup_<statename>`.

2. Drag-and-drop an instance of the `TriviaCardScript` to the **GameObject**. Set the card width and height to `320,320`.

3. Drag-and-drop an instance of `SimpleLifespanScript` to the **GameObject**. Set the seconds parameter to `4`. This will make sure that if the information card disappears, it does not matter if you toggle it off from the inventory or if the user just lets it time out naturally.

4. Repeat steps 1 to 3 for each of the 50 states.

5. Drag-and-drop a reference to each of these Prefabs to the appropriate `flagObject` Prefab. Note that the reference for the game information pop up is in the `CustomGameInfo` component of the `flag` object.

Congratulations! You have now created the learning content for the first level of the game. If you need to update these, simply edit the textures in your pixel art program, and Unity3D will naturally update the code and Prefabs.

Creating the mission pop-up Prefab

These game missions communicate their state to the user through pop ups. We need to create two more special purposes dialog boxes that the game will use to reward the user and to inform the user of what the next objective is in the game. The first one, named returnFlagsToMonument, communicates to the user that they have all five flags and should walk back to the monument to finish. The second one, named Level1Done, communicates that the level is done and that the next level will load.

We can create a mission pop-up Prefab by performing the following steps:

1. Create a new GUITexture object, and name it returnFlagsToMonument.

2. Drag-and-drop an instance of the TriviaCardScript to the GameObject. Set the card width and height to 320,320.

3. Drag-and-drop an instance of the TriviaCardScript to the GameObject. Set the card width and height to 320,320.

4. Drag-and-drop an instance of SimpleLifespanScript to the GameObject. Set the seconds parameter to 4. This will make sure the pop up disappears after it times out.

5.   Repeat steps 1 to 3 for another texture named Level1Done.

Congratulations! These two Prefabs will be used to communicate the user's progress through the learning objectives in level one. Create Prefabs by dragging-and-dropping these GameObjects to the project tab. We will place these Prefabs into the missionMgr script to finish configuring the level.

Creating the mission reward Prefabs

By exploiting the fact that a GameObject Prefab can contain any number of sub-objects in the hierarchy, we can create Prefabs with any number of results to be achieved in the world when a mission is complete. We will use this fact to aggregate and pack together all of the results we want to achieve when the user accomplishes their goals. We will use this fact to construct a reward for when the flags are all found and a separate reward for when the flags are returned to the monument.

Creating the FoundAllTheFlags Prefab

The FoundAllTheFlags Prefab can be created by performing the following steps:

1.   Create a new GUITexture object, and name it returnFlagsToMonument.

2.   Drag-and-drop an instance of the returnFlagsToMonument Prefab to this object.

3.   Create a new **Cube** GameObject, and name it FlagReturnTriggerObj. This object will be an invisible InteractiveObj class that will (on being picked up by the user), add the final token to the inventory, which will satisfy the second mission in the level.

4. Scale and position it so that it rests on top of the monument. Give it a large height, and make it about 15 percent wider and deeper than the monument itself. Add this object to the `FoundAllTheFlags` object.

5. Disable the mesh renderer on this object so that we no longer see it.

6. Add `MissionToken` to this object, give it an ID of `10`. Give it a title `ReturnToBase` and an appropriate description, such as `Returns Flags To Base`.

7. Add an object interaction script. Set the interaction to `AddMissionToken`, and set the **interactionType** to `Unique`.

8. Add an `InteractiveObj` class, and set the `OnCloseEnough` script reference to the `ObjectInteractionScipt` from this object!

9. Drag this object to the project tab to create a Prefab from it.

Congratulations! Now, when this parent object (`FoundAllTheFlags` Prefab) is instantiated, the following will occur:

- The `returnFlagsToMonument` Prefab will be instantiated. This object will detach itself from the parent and display the pop-up GUITexture for a few seconds before destroying itself.

- The `FlagReturnTriggerObj` Prefab will be instantiated. This invisible object will sit at the top of the monument. When the user walks back to the monument, this will result in a new mission token being collected, which will activate the second mission and complete the level!

Creating the ReturnedTheFlagsResult Prefab

One other Prefab is needed to finish the logic for level one. This Prefab will be instantiated once the user has gotten all the five objects and returned them to the monument.

1. Create a new, empty **GameOobject**, place it at (`0,0,0`), and name it `ReturnedTheFlagsResult`.

2. Add an instance of the `Level1Done` Prefab (that displays the pop-up dialog box for level completed) as a child of `ReturnedTheFlagsResult`.

3. Create a new, empty **GameObject**, name it `InventoryPlaceAllFlags`, and add it as a child of `ReturnedTheFlagsResult`.

4. Add five instances of the `InventoryPlaceOnMonument` script to this object. Set each one to a unique `ObjectIndex` from **0** to **4**. This will remove a single object from the inventory and attach it to the monument at the flag mount of the same index.

5. Drag this Prefab back into the project tab to make a Prefab from this compound object.

Congratulations! Now when this parent object (`ReturnedTheFlagsResult`) is instantiated, the following will occur:

- The pop-up Prefab will be instantiated. This object will detach itself from the parent, and display the pop-up GUITexture for a few seconds before destroying itself.

- The `FlagReturnTriggerObj` Prefab will be instantiated. This invisible object will sit at the top of the monument. When the user walks back to the monument, it will result in a new mission token being collected, which will activate the second mission and complete the level!

Configuring the mission manager

Before we can test our game level, we need to configure the `MissionMgr` class. This class acts as the dispatcher and gate for the dynamic behavior of the game logic. It can be configured by performing the following steps:

1. Ensure that there are two missions in `MissionMgr`; the size of the missions list in the mission manager is equal to 2.

2. Generally, the default values inside a mission don't really matter (since we set them up in custom scripts such as `SetupMissionOne.cs`; however, some values need to be preconfigured).

3. In the second mission (mission one), make sure that the token array is of size 1, and has a reference to the `FlagReturnTriggerObj` mission token on the `InteractiveObject` class that is sitting on top of the `MissionMgr` script.

4. In the first mission, set the reward reference variable to the `foundtheflagresult` Prefab in the project tab.

5. In the second mission, set the reward reference variable to the `returnedtheflagsresult` Prefab in the project tab.

And that's it! Now when these two missions are finished, those Prefabs will be instanced, causing pop ups to appear and time out, and causing other interactions with the inventory and missions systems as discussed previously.

Playing the level!

We can test our work now by playing the level! Drive the player around the level to find the five missing flags. Once found, press their icon in the inventory to read the information about each state. Once all five flags are found, the system will tell you to return them to the monument, at which time the flags will return and the mission will be done.

Summary

We have shown how to apply the `Player`, `InteractiveObj`, `ObjectInteraction`, `InventoryMgr`, and `MissionMgr` classes that we developed in the first two chapters to create a fun "collect-and-interact" mechanic system for our e-learning game. We also reviewed a model of fun and "gamification" and how this model can be used in e-learning games to design content that will present and encourage consolidation of learning objectives in the user.

Going forward, we will review our code thus far, and make some maintenance changes to future proof the code, ensuring we can extend it and that it will remain suitable for subsequent e-learning games with a different content.

4
Mission One – Future Proofing the Code

We have designed and implemented a working first pass on the first mission of our game. Take a moment to step back and celebrate! To make sure we can finish creating the last two levels and finish polishing this level, we will need to revisit some of the code we have already written to ensure it is extensible to meet the needs of the other two missions in our game.

We will restructure the existing game into a number of subscenes. Then we will reintegrate the code so that the game can support multiple scene files; hence, it will support multiple levels. We will extend our interactive object system so that it supports more general purpose operations with transforms, which are necessary for future mission requirements. Finally, we will finish the trivia cards with an eye towards testing and application for the last levels.

In this chapter, we will cover the following topics:

- Reorganizing our GameObjects in the **Scene** view
- Adding new scenes to the project
- Creating the `PopupMainMenu` GameObject
- An introduction to Finite State Machines
- Implementing the `GameMgr` script
- Reflecting on our code changes
- Analyzing of code functionality
- Updating some systems

Reorganizing our GameObjects in the Scene view

The following GameObjects will be the focus of our design activities in this chapter:

- GameMgr: This script will handle the choreography between the game and its particular states. It will hold the logic that moves the game from the main screen and between the individual levels.

- PlayerData: This script will hold the game instance-specific attributes of the player. This will include variables such as score and current level.

- Game: This is the GameObject that holds the scripts necessary for game control. It will hold the GameMgr script as well as the MissionMgr script.

- _level1: This class will hold all of the objects that are specific to the first level.

- _global: This class will hold all of the objects that are global or persistent across all game levels as shown in the following screenshot:

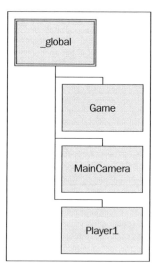

Taking an already working system of code and reworking it so that it is more extendible is called **Refactoring**. By refactoring our game into a number of scene files, we will find that the game becomes easier to extend and maintain. This is important for us to be able to add new lessons and levels to the game.

Previously, our approach to game programming in Unity was to place all
`GameObject` instances inside one scene file. This worked because the lifespan
of all GameObjects was the same—the duration of the whole program.

In a multilevel game, we will want to keep some objects persistent for the
entire lifespan of the program. Other objects, we will want to only use during a
particular level, and perhaps we may want some objects only fleetingly during a
particular level.

Let's separate our work thus far into two scene files: one for persistent objects and
one for level-one-specific objects.

Creating a global scene

The global scene file will contain all persistent GameObjects and scripts that have a
lifespan of the entire game. To create this file, perform the following steps:

1. Create a new empty GameObject, and name it `_global`.

2. Set its position to (`0`, `0`, `0`). Doing this before we drag-and-drop objects
    beneath it will ensure that the world space positions of the child objects
    will stay the same as they were previously.

3. Drag-and-drop the following GameObjects beneath the `_global`
    GameObject. These will eventually be moved to a new scene file
    named `MAIN` as shown in the following screenshot.

    ○ `MainCamera`

    ○ `MissionMgr`

    ○ `Player`

4. Rename `MissionMgr` to `Game`. We rename it because we are expanding the
    responsibilities of this object beyond just `MissionMgr`; we will be adding
    another script to this object to increase its responsibilities in the game, so a
    more generic name is appropriate.

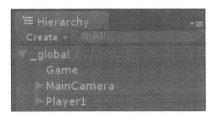

5. Create a new script, and name it `GameMgr`. Attach it to the object named `Game`.
    We will implement this script later in this chapter.

6.   Create a new script, and name it `PlayerData`. Attach it to the object named `Game`. We will implement this script later in this chapter.

7.   Create a new scene by selecting **New Scene** from the **File** drop-down menu. This will be the new starting scene for our game going forward. Name it `MAIN`.

8.   Switch back to the `CHAPTER3_SCENE1` scene file. Copy the `_global` GameObject from the **Hierarchy** tab by either right-clicking on it and selecting **Copy** or by clicking on the object and pressing *Ctrl + C*.

9.   Switch to the `MAIN` scene again, and paste the `_global` object into this scene by pressing *Ctrl + V*.

Congratulations! We have created a scene file that will act as the launcher for our new game framework. Let's repeat the process for the first level.

Creating a first level scene

The `LEVEL1` scene file will contain all transient GameObjects and scripts that have a lifespan for just the first level of the game. The level one scene will look like the following screenshot:

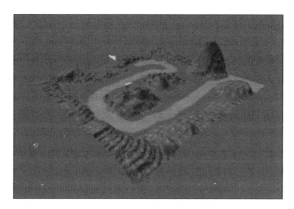

To create the first-level scene, perform the following steps:

1.   Create a new, empty GameObject, and name it `_level1`.

2.   Set its position to (`0, 0, 0`). Doing this before we drag-and-drop objects beneath it will ensure that the world space positions of the child objects will stay the same as they were previously.

3.   Switch back to scene `Chapter3_Scene1`. Drag-and-drop the following game objects beneath the `_level1` GameObject:

      ◦   `Directional light`

- ◦ FlagLocators
- ◦ Monument
- ◦ Terrain

4. Create a new scene by navigating to **File | New Scene** from the drop-down menu. This will be the scene for our first level going forward. Name it LEVEL1.

5. Switch back to the CHAPTER3_SCENE1 level. Copy the _level1 GameObject from the **Hierarchy** tab by either right clicking on it and selecting **Copy** or by selecting the object and pressing *Ctrl + C*.

6. Switch to the LEVEL1 scene again, and paste the _level1 object into this scene by pressing *Ctrl + V*.

Congratulations! We now have a second scene file that will correspond to the game content for level one. Now we need to make sure that these levels are added the project.

Adding new scenes to the project

In order to ensure these scenes are available to the game project, we need to add them to the build as shown in the following screenshot:

To add the scenes to the build, perform the following steps:

1. Double-click on the **MAIN** scene in the project tab. Once it is loaded, select **Build Settings** from the **File** drop-down menu, and notice that the previous pop-up window appears. Once there, click on the **Add Current** button; observe now that a new scene file name has been added to the **scenes in build** window.

2. Repeat this process for LEVEL1 as well as for CHAPTER3_SCENE1, CHAPTER2_SCENE1, and CHAPTER1_SCENE1. While we don't need the last three in our final build, let's add them so that they are available for convenience.

Congratulations! Now these new scenes will be accessible to the game. Let's connect the new level one scene to the main scene file with a simple pop up.

Creating the PopupMainMenu GameObject

A great game requires an interesting and usable user interface system. Our game will require a number of pop-up windows that will be used to communicate to the user. The user will also be able to interact with the game by selecting buttons on pop ups. The first pop up we need to create is the one that starts the game on the main menu.

A number of middleware technologies exist to help the Unity developer create active UI systems quickly and with high quality; at the time of writing this book, NGUI and EGUI are pop-up systems available on the Unity asset store for this very purpose. While it is possible to use any one of these or other extensions to build your UI, we will develop our own from scratch. Let's create a start screen from which we will launch level one by performing the following steps:

1. Switch to the MAIN scene file.

2. Create a plane, and parent it to MainCamera. This will serve as the background to our pop-up window panel.

3. Set its position to (0, 0, 0), and orient it towards the camera. Translate it along its z axis so that it is forward from the camera by 9 units.

4. Scale the plane by 1.5 on the x axis, and rotate it to 270 degrees around the x axis. At this point, the plane should move with the camera and occlude its line of sight to the rest of the scene. Now, by enabling this GameObject, we have a fullscreen backdrop for menus. Name this plane PopupMainMenu.

5. Create a new, colored material, and apply it to the plane. In our example, I selected the green color.

6. Create a 3D text object. Notice that the component is named `TextMesh`. This will be used to communicate with the user in our simple menu page. Parent it to `PopupMainMenu`. Set its relative position to (-3.3, 0.8, 2.9) so that it is near the top and centered. Set its scale to (0.6, 1, 1), and apply a 90 degree rotation to the *x* axis so that it is nicely centered at the top of the screen.

7. Note that the `TextMesh` component in the inspector is a container for the 3DText specific parameters. Set the text to the name of our game Geography Quest.

8. Set the **CharacterSize** to 0.5 and the **FontSize** to 21 to make the title appear with an appealing size and shape. Just as one might do with a word processor, set the font style to bold for extra visual impact.

9. Name this 3DText object `textGeographyQuest` to keep the hierarchy easy to read and maintain.

10. Now, we need a prompt for the user to click to start. Let's duplicate the previous GameObject by clicking on it and pressing *Ctr + D*.

11. Rename this object `textClickToContinue`. Set the text field of the `TextMesh` on this object to `New`.

12. Move the GameObject to (-1.8, 0.9, 1.2), and scale the font size down to 15 to place and scale the text appropriately.

13. Our menu is almost complete! Let's write a script to handle the mouse-click event. Create a new script, and name it `MainMenuScript`. Attach this script to the `PopupMainMenu` object.

14. This script will have two private member variables. One to store the main Game GameObject (the one that holds the `GameMgr` and `MissionMgr` classes) and one to hold the `GameMgr` script instance itself (attached to `Game`). We make these private because the object being referred to doesn't need to change during the lifespan of the game, so finding it automatically on startup is more robust. They can be configured as shown in the following code:

```
private GameMgr gm;
Private GameObject GameObj;
```

15. Inside the `Start()` method, we will search for the object named `Game`. If it is found, we store a reference to the `GameMgr` script instance attached to this object as shown in the following code. Recall that the `Start()` method gets invoked by the Unity engine for any class that inherits from `MonoBehavior` the first time it runs after instantiation:

```
GameObj = GameObject.Find("Game");
if (GameObj)
{
  gm = GameObj.GetComponent<GmeMgr>();
};
```

16. We now implement a method to handle the mouse click as shown in the following code. Unity will automatically invoke a method called `OnMouseDown()` when the user clicks the mouse, so we will use that for detecting the click. This is one of many methods that the `MonoBehavior` base class provides for new C# scripts that you create in Unity3D with the new script wizard:

```
void OnMouseDown() { };
```

17. Inside this method, if we have a `GameMgr` script reference, then we will do two things. We call `gm.SetState()`, and change the state to `eGameState.eGS_Level1` as shown in the following code. This enumeration is defined inside of the `GameMgr` class and corresponds to the game being in level one. We will investigate how `GameMgr` handles this next. Of course, `gm` will only be defined if we remember to rename the `MissionMgr` to `Game` as requested earlier in this chapter:

```
gm.SetState(gameMgr.eGameState.eGS_Level1);
```

18. We also then set the `GameObject` active flag to `false`. This causes the object to cease to update. No scripts or components attached to `PopupMainMenu` will run until `active` is set to `true` again. This has the effect of disabling the pop up (which is what we will want).

Congratulations! This pop up will be created when the `MAIN` scene is loaded, and when clicked, it will tell the `GameMgr` to change levels to level one.

An introduction to Finite State Machines

A common strategy in game play programming (and computer science in general) is to model a system in terms of discrete objects and their interactions with one another. To do this requires us to understand what the participants are in a system, how they operate in different scenarios, and how they change states.

The **Finite State Machine (FSM)** is one such technique. With this, the idea is to model the behavior of the object in a number of code blocks. Inside each one, you put the specific code for that block that makes it unique. You also determine what scenarios cause an object to switch from one block (state) to another. Because each state is an encapsulation, it makes your code extensible and maintainable (which is a great thing!).

Implementing an FSM in a game

While there are many ways of programming an FSM, we will commonly encounter two strategies as game programmers on our e-learning example. Each one has its own unique structural components, benefits, and drawbacks.

The switch case FSM

In this form, we require three components:

- An enumeration to list the states: Each individual element in the enumerated type corresponds to a single state in the FSM model. For example, an FSM with three states could be implemented in the enumeration eMyState as shown in the following code:

```
public enum eMyState {
  STATE_INVALD = -1, // an error state which can be used to
    encode the logic for processing an error condition
  STATE_A = 0, // an arbitrary state in an FSM
  STATE_B = 1, // a second arbitrary state
  STATE_C = 2 // a third arbitrary state, et cetera
};
```

  Note that we make the enumeration public so that other client classes can have access (to set the state). Also note that we have four distinct states for an FSM with three logical states as it is useful to encode an error state in our type for -1. A variable of type eMyState is declared in the class to store the current value of the state.

- A switch case block: This structure allows the program to jump to the current state/block (as indicated from the enumeration) to invoke the code for that state as shown in the following code:

```
Switch (state) {
  case(eMyState.STATE_A):
  {
    // code for STATE A here
    break;
  }

  case(eMyState.STATE_B):
  {
    // code for STATE B here
    break;
  }

  case(eMyState.STATE_C):
  {
```

```
   // code for STATE C here
   break;
}

Default:
{
   // handle fatal error
   break;
}
}
```

- A system for encoding and switching state: Two variables of type eMyState are used. One to encode current state and one to encode previous tick state. The previous tick state updates itself to current state on every frame of the update loop. When the current state is not the same as the previous tick state, it means that we have changed state and need to update the current state var:

```
if (gameState != _prevGameState)
{
   ChangeState(gameState);
}
_prevGameState = gameState;
```

Classes implementation of FSM

In this second form of FSM, an individual C# class is used for each state. This class's update loop then holds the body of the code for that state's specialization. Changing states is performed the same way as in the previous example. An enumeration is also used to give other systems in the codebase a means of setting states.

Implementing the GameMgr script

Let's implement the GameMgr script so that it can manage the loading (and future unloading) of scene files and assets. Implementing this in a flexible way now will make our game more extensible when we have future levels to add. It can be implemented by performing the following steps:

1. Recall that we have already created an empty script named GameMgr and attached it to the Game GameObject. If you have not already done this, no worries; just create a new script now, and attach it.

2. In order for GameMgr to do its job, it will act as a mediator between popupMenu and the scene files of the game. When GameMgr receives a message to change its state, it will load and unload the appropriate scene files.

3. It is important that at this point we have added the LEVEL1 scene file to the build settings; if you have not yet done this, make sure it has been added now.

4. We will use a custom enumeration in this class to build a state machine. This is a data structure that will let us build a model of how all scene files in the game interact with one another (which loads first, which stays persistent, which loads next, and so on). For complex systems later in the game, we will use this concept repeatedly.

5. We add an entry for both scene files we have created as well as a special error value that we can use to trap potential data problems. Extending this enumeration is as simple as adding more entries to this structure and assigning new entries a new unique integer as shown in the following code:

```
public enum eGameState
{
  eGS_Invalid = -1, //used to encode error condition when
    setting gamestate
  eGS_MainMenu = 0,//a state to encode being in the mainmenu
  eGS_Level1 = 1//a state to encode being in level1
}
```

6. For GameMgr to be able to detect when a state change occurs, we will require two variables: one for the GameState and one for the GameState on the previous time the Update() loop ran. By checking each frame if the GameState has changed, we can detect when to load a new level as shown in the following code:

```
public eGameState gameState;
private eGameState _prevGameState;
```

While we don't want the user to be able to set prevGameState ever from the inspector, we allow the GameState to be adjusted by the user for debugging purposes.

7. In the Start() method of this class, we initialize GameState and prevGameState to the same value as shown in the following code. With an initial value of eGS_MainMenu, this corresponds to the main menu scene (which is the one we will default to when we load the MAIN scene). How convenient! Note that since both the previous and current GameStates are the same, GameMgr will not try and load a new scene file right away:

```
GameState = eGameState.eGS_MainMenu
prevGameState = eGameState.eGS_MainMenu;
```

8. We create a public method to allow other systems to set the state as shown in the following code. By ensuring that we always use this function rather than assigning to state directly, it will allow us to change state to private later on (once the game is done) without having to change the code elsewhere:

```
public void SetState(eGameState gs)
{
   GameState = gs;
}
```

9. In the Update() loop, the code will check if GameState is not equal to prevGameState. When this happens, it means that in this frame, the GameState was changed by another system and that GameMgr should change levels. To perform the state change, the code will invoke a custom private method ChangeState() as shown in the following code:

```
void Update() {
    if (GameState != prevGameState)
    {
        ChangeState(gameState);
    }
    prevGameState = GameState;
}
```

10. The ChangeState() method checks the current game state (guaranteed to have just changed this frame) as shown in the following code. We use a switch statement to handle selection of conditional logic based on the value of the new, current game state. Switch is a variation on the compound if/else structure you may have seen before; when there are multiple options to select from, switch is regarded by many as being easier to read and maintain:

```
GameState = gs;
switch(gameState)
```

11. We don't need to do anything at this point for the case where we switch states to MainMenu (since we only allow this state on start by default). Recall that PopupMainMenu switches to LEVEL1 GameState on click. We handle this by calling Application.LoadLevelAdditive("LEVEL1"). This line of code loads the scene file by name (so long as it has been added to the build) and adds all of the game objects from that scene to the current scene. The net result of this will be a scene file with two game objects at the top level; _global (and all of its children) and _level1 (and all of its children). Since we never duplicate objects between scene files, we now have a complete playable scene as shown in the following code:

```
case(eGameState.eGS_Level1):
{
    Application.LoadLevelAdditive("LEVEL1");
    break;
};
```

If you have Unity3D Pro, you can replace `Application.LoadLevelAdditive()` with `Application.LoadLevelAdditiveAsync()`, which will make the level transition appear smoother for large levels (since it doesn't block the renderer). If you accidentally use `LoadLevelAsync()` or `LoadLevel()`, you will find that the objects that were previously loaded will be deleted when the new level loads up (possibly `_global` and its children in our case).

Congratulations! We now have written a game state manager class `GameMgr`, which uses the mediator pattern to selective load scene files that correspond to different levels in our game.

Reflecting on our code changes

Before we can test our code properly, let's reflect on what we have done. While we have made our game framework more flexible and extensible, we have also broken some assumptions from before that need repairing as discussed in the following points:

- The `MissionManager` class has been renamed to `Game`. This means that all scripts that used to do a `GameObject.Find("MissionManager")` need to be updated to `Find("Game")`.

- We have separated some objects into the MAIN scene and some into the LEVEL1 scene. This means that objects that have a reference to an object that is now in another scene will be broken. To repair these, we need to modify the code for the object in the scene. See `SetupSceneOne` for an example of this.

Analyzing code functionality

We can test our work now by switching to the MAIN scene file and clicking on
Play. Notice right off the bat that there is one **GameObject** in the **Hierarchy** view,
the _global object that holds the main camera, the Game, and the Player. We should
also see the main menu pop up right away as shown in the following screenshot:

Clicking anywhere on the pop up sends a message to GameMgr to switch the level to
Level1. Upon doing so, we should notice two GameObjects in the hierarchy view:
the _global object and the level1 object (which has the terrain, monument, flag
holders, and directional light) as shown in the following screenshot. By using this
structure of relating the scene name to the name of a game object at the root of the
project view, we will make unloading of levels really easy.

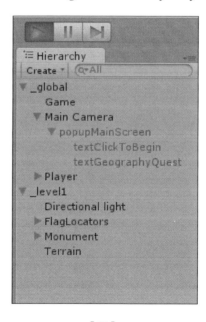

Updating some systems

We introduce a new class, `PlayerData`, to track the current level and points accrued of the player. To make use of this new functionality, we need to update some systems by performing the following steps:

1. Switch to the LEVEL1 scene. Double-click on the `PlayerData` script to begin editing it.

2. Add a `public int score` and a `public GameState` level; note that in order to create an instance of the enumeration defined inside the `GameMgr` class, we need to prefix with `GameMgr` as shown in the following code:

```
public class playerData : MonoBehaviour {
public int score;
public GameMgr eGameState;
```

3. Add a public method called `addScore(int dScore)`. This method will be used by the different systems (primarily `MissionMgr`), to add score to the player's record. Note that since we use an integer for score, we could use this same method to add score or penalize the player (by adding negative scores) as shown in the following code:

```
public void AddScore(int dScore)
{
   score += dScore;
}
```

4. Add a public method called `StoreProgress(gameMgr.eGameState lvl)`. This method will be used to track which level the user is currently trying to complete. We declare the method public rather than private so that other classes will be allowed to invoke this method on an instance of the `PlayerData` component. If it were private, then the code would not compile as shown in the following code:

```
public void StoreProgres{gameMgr.eGameState lvl)
{
   level = lvl;
} ;
```

Now, let's connect the score tracking to the points in the game. Recall that `MissionMgr` stores a points field for each mission once it is completed. Let's go to `MissionMgr` and modify it to add the completed mission points to the `PlayerData` component.

5. In `MissionMgr`, in the `Validate()` method, let's add a code block that searches for the `PlayerData` component on the `Player` GameObject. If it is found, then the points from the mission are added to the `PlayerData` score as shown in the following code:

```
GameObject go = GameObject.Find("Player1");
if (go)
{
    PlayerData pd = go.GetComponent<PlayerData>();
    if (pd)
        pd.AddScore(m.points);
}
```

6. In order to visualize the player's score, let's add a `guiText` script to the bottom-right corner of the screen to show the score. To begin, create a new `guiText` script.

7. Name this object `score`. Parent it to the `_global` GameObject (because it should have persistency in the game). Set its position to (1, 1, 0) to offset the coordinates of the pixel-offset to the upper-right corner of the screen. This way, the negative *x* and *y* components of the pixel-offset will offset the score from the corner by the specified amount. Set **x** to `-60` and **y** to `-20`.

Making the ScorePlate active

Let's create a simple script to update the text field of this score as shown in the following screenshot:

The following script will update the text field in the upper-right corner of the screen so that it reflects the score stored in PlayerData:

1. Switch to the **MAIN** scene. Create a new script, and name it `scoreScript.cs`.

2. Attach an instance of this script to the `score` GameObject.

3. In the start method of this script, find the GameObject named `Player`, and then store a reference to the `PlayerData` component on this script.

4. The `score` script needs to update a member of the `GUIText` GameObject `score`, so the update loop that this script should be called from is `OnGUI()`. Inside this loop, we check for a `PlayerData` component as shown in the following code:

    ```
    void OnGUI() { }
    GameObject go = GameObject.Find("Player")
    ```

5. If there is one, we take the score value from `PlayerData` and assign it to the text field of the textbox. Note that we have to use the C# helper function `.ToString()` to convert the integer score value to a string that the GUIText can use as shown in the following code:

    ```
    if (pd)
    {
        int score = pd.GetScore();
        this.gameObject.GetComponent<GUIText>().text =
        score.ToString();
    }
    ```

Congratulations! Now, if we switch back to the MAIN scene and playtest, note that once you have collected five flags, the score updates to 500. Return the flags to the monument for another 500 points!

Updating the player motion algorithm

To make our game character move through the level more smoothly, we will modify the motion algorithm. Instead of relying on gravity on the rigid body to keep the player anchored to the ground, we will cast a ray downward and glue the player to the polygon directly below. In this way, the curvature of the terrain will play less of a role in restricting the player. This can be achieved by performing the following steps:

1. Switch to the MAIN scene, and double click on the `PlayerControls` script on the player. In the `UpdateMovement()` method, directly after the `CharacterController.Move()` method is called, declare a `RayCastHit` class named `hitInfo` as shown in the following code. This class will be used to return the position of the polygon from a raycast that is directly below the player. By invoking a raycast downward, we can check what other GameObject is intersected and use this information to glue the player to the ground directly at the point of contact:

   ```
   RayCastHit hitInfo;
   ```

2. We create a new ray that points straight down from the player. We use the player's transform to determine the downward direction rather than the world transform so that even if the player is rotated, the raycast will always look down relative to the character as shown in the following code:

   ```
   Ray r = new Ray(this.transform.position, -Vector3.up);
   ```

3. We query the physics system by casting the previous ray and allowing the PhysX integration to return the polygon that this raycast has hit, through the `hitinfo` variable, as shown in the following code:

   ```
   Physics.Raycast( r, out hitinfo);
   ```

4. Finally, we set the **y** position of the character to the **y** position of the poly that was hit in the raycast, plus an offset. We do this by creating a `new Vector3` variable to assign to the `transform.position` variable as we cannot assign to just a single component of this value type. The offset that we use to raise the character in the **y** direction is the height of the player's collision capsule as shown in the following code:

   ```
   this.transform.position = new
     Vector3(this.transform.position.x, hitinfo.point.y +
     (this.collider as CapsuleCollider).height,
     this.transform.position.z);
   ```

Playing the level!

We can test our work now by playing the level. Start the level by running the MAIN scene. Notice the main menu pop-up window that presents the game and waits for the player to click to begin. Once level one loads, drive the player around the level to find the five missing flags. Once found, press their icon in the inventory to read the information about each state as these information card Prefabs have now been updated with interesting trivia about each region. Once all five are found, the system will tell you to return them to the monument, at which time the flags will return, and the mission will be done. Note the score updating when each mission is updated and the smooth character motion across the terrain.

Summary

We have engaged in an iteration on our game program and refactored the working level from the last chapter into multiple scenes. We have created a GameMgr class to handle the new game states for our game, and we have associated individual level scenes with unique states; a good practice for flexible and extensible programming. We updated the camera, score, and PlayerData systems to add further polish and functionality to our game. Next, we will learn about the various user interface options that Unity provides. We will use these to develop a HUD system for our game that will meet the final needs of our e-learning game.

5
User Interfaces in Unity

To provide the level of polish necessary for commercial applications, Unity offers a variety of user interface systems to the game programmer. Understanding what each of these systems is designed to do, what each is good at, and how to combine them, will enable the programmer to build retail class menus, navigation buttons, and more.

In this chapter, we will investigate, analyze, and understand these systems. We will then apply this knowledge and build an extensible pop-up system using Prefabs for commonly used scenarios in our game. We will finish by integrating these into mission one with an eye on future missions and future extensibility. In this chapter, we will cover the following topics:

- Getting familiar with the Unity UI classes
- Developing the pop-up system
- Exploring the `GUIText` component
- Exploring the `GUITexture` component
- Exploring the `TextMesh` component
- Creating clickable text elements
- UnityScript and the `GUI Button` object
- Building the main menu pop up
- Testing our work
- Future extensions

Getting familiar with Unity UI classes

We will cover the following Unity UI systems:

- `GUIText`: This component displays a 2D font in screen space. It is well suited for the in-game HUD text that stays relatively stationary on the screen. It is displayed in screen-relative coordinates.

- `GUITexture`: This component displays a 2D image in screen space. It is well suited for the background and border graphics for in-game HUD elements. Just as the preceding component, this component is also displayed in screen-relative coordinates.

- `TextMesh`: This component generates a 3D mesh for a given string and displays it in the game world in 3D coordinates. This mesh can be positioned and oriented for in-game-specific purposes. This makes it suitable for displaying the text on the screen at a size that is invariant to the screen resolution.

- `GUIButton`: The Unity Engine offers a script-only API for generating user interface buttons. These are suitable for 2D elements that need to be animated in screen space and for the dynamic menu UI in the game. These elements cannot be placed in the editor like the other classes discussed earlier in this list; they are controlled entirely from within C#.

Developing the pop-up system

As a case study, we will apply our knowledge of the systems described earlier as we build the following Prefabs. The pop-up system will consist of a window that can display text and graphics. An instance of a pop up can have a number of buttons, each of which will interact with the game in an easy-to-program way. We will integrate them into our existing mission one to achieve a higher level of polish, and these will form the new active user interface, which the user will use to communicate with the game, and with which the game will communicate with the user.

- `popupMenu`: This pop-up Prefab will provide the usability for an in-game menu system. It will have clickable buttons for the user to interact with.

- `popupInfo`: This class will present information about the game to the user, with a single button to interact with.

Exploring the GUIText component

The easiest way to display text on screen in a camera-relative way is through the
GUIText component. To use this component, you need to add an instance of this
component to an existing game object in your scene, and set the text field to the
string you want to display.

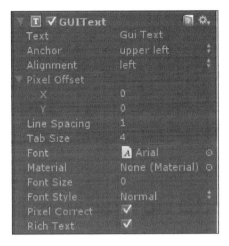

Please keep in mind that the way in which the transform component of the GUIText
GameObject is processed for GUIText is different for other GameObjects with the
same component, which we will discuss later.

Interpreting the members on GUIText

A (0.5, 0.5, 0.0f) position corresponds to the center of the screen. For this
component to work as designed, the object needs to be placed here in the world.
The x and y components of the (x, y, z) vector on the transform range from 0.0f to
1.0f each.

Do not place GUIText on a moving object. If the transform moves, the
meaning of the text position will change, and the text will likely go some
place you don't want it to! If you want to track a moving object with
GUIText, then you need to adjust the x and y values in the **Pixel Inset**
vector instead of parenting it.

The **Pixel Inset** vector is a special 2D vector that specifies where on the screen (relative to the transform's x, y components) the text should be displayed. The units of this are in pixels and not screen percentages. This means that if you resize your window, these numbers may not remain correct. The fix for this is to set your pixel offsets via a script.

The **Anchor** and **Alignment** fields on the **GUIText** component correspond to the location where the position should be tracked on the string itself. With options in the center or at the corners, the API allows the programmer to easily align the text field at the center or the margin.

The **Font Size** and **Font Style** fields allow the programmer to specify the size of the text and whether it should be rendered normal, bold, or italic. Use these liberally to give your text some added visual pop and personality.

The **Font** field is where the actual font file reference for this text is established. By importing various fonts into Unity, you can render your 2D text in a variety of typesets.

Exploring the GUITexture component

As we can now display 2D text, let's discuss how we can add visually appealing graphics to our interfaces; the GUITexture component does precisely this. You can see the **GUITexture** component as follows:

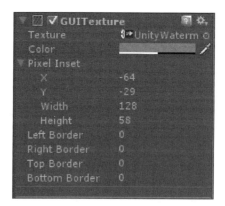

The **Texture** field is a reference to a 2D graphic element. This could be a .png, .jpg, or .bmp file that you created in the Paint program on your computer. Each file type has its benefits and drawbacks depending on how much compression you need in your file. Dragging-and-dropping it into the **Project** tab will import the image, after which you can set the reference.

The **Color** field lets the user select a specific tint for the GUITexture. This is a convenient way to fine-tune the appearance of the texture without having to edit it in your external Paint program.

The **Pixel Inset** field works in a way similar to the **Pixel Offset** field. The **X** and **Y** fields correspond to the screen space coordinates of the upper-left corner of the texture. The **Width** and **Height** fields provide a way to stretch and scale the graphics vertically and horizontally; combining these two lets the programmer place and resize the visuals precisely.

The **Left Border**, **Right Border**, **Top Border**, and **Bottom Border** fields provide a way to tile the texture to the left, right, top, or bottom of the original. These measurements are in pixels as well and not in screen percentages.

To make sure that the GUITexture component you create displays behind the GUIText that you instantiate, you can adjust their relative priorities with the **Z** component of the transform position. Larger z components will draw closer to the camera and smaller ones (even negative ones) will draw farther away. Keeping this in mind, we can sort our textures and text elements as required by our design.

Exploring the TextMesh component

The TextMesh user interface component operates differently than the previous two components. It actually generates a polygonal mesh based on the text rather than display a 2D font or 2D texture. It then places the mesh at the location and orientation specified in the GameObject's transform. This means that we can place this mesh directly in the game world!

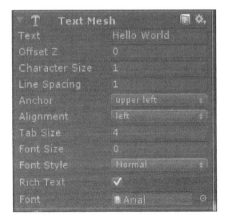

Ideal use of TextMesh

One of the useful applications of TextMesh is that it can be placed in the world at its transform position. This makes it adept at labeling objects that move around the world. This can be done by parenting the TextMesh component to the GameObject, with a slight vertical offset in the TextMesh transform.

Creating clickable text elements

To process whether any of the preceding elements have been clicked or not by the mouse pointer, we have to manually program the handling of this event. Luckily for us, since these components are attached to a GameObject (which inherits from MonoBehavior), we can use mouse events that MonoBehavior provides.

Detecting mouse clicks

Whenever the mouse pointer is clicked while the pointer is over the top of a GameObject, the OnMouseDown callback is invoked. With this, we can trap these button clicks and respond accordingly:

```
void OnMouseDown() { // insert code here }
```

Detecting mouse over

A second callback method is called whenever the mouse pointer moves onto a GameObject. This function is a convenient way to handle the highlighting of the GUI elements when they are selected or browsed:

```
void OnMouseOver() { // insert code here }
```

Detecting leaving mouse over

A final callback method is called whenever the mouse leaves from over the top of a GameObject. This is the complement of the preceding mouseOver handler and can be used in conjunction with the preceding method of turning highlighting on and off:

```
void OnMouseExit() { // insert code here }
```

Exploring UnityScript and the GUIButton object

The Unity Editor is laid out with an internal GUI-specification language called UnityGUI. This API is only accessible to Unity game programmers from within C# (and JavaScript) code, unlike the previous GUI elements that can be placed and adjusted within the editor itself at design time. We can use this to place buttons, textures, pop-up windows, tooltips, and many other UI primitives. The difference in use from the previous examples is that the elements are instanced and placed entirely from the script rather than at design time in the editor. For our dialog pop-up Prefabs, we will explore the GUI.Button class.

Using UnityGUI

To use the UnityGUI functionality, we must invoke the commands from within a special callback, OnGUI(). As this function is not created by default when you create a new C# script in Unity, you need to add it yourself. The Unity Engine will invoke this method automatically when GUI elements are to be redrawn; so, we put our GUIButton code and GUITexture and GUIText update code in here:

```
void OnGUI() { // insert code here }
```

Creating a clickable button

To create a button, use the GUI namespace and instantiate a button with parameters into the constructor. There are six different function signatures one can use to instantiate a GUI button, depending on which visuals or string you want to display on it. Each type, however, requires the rect class as the first parameter:

```
GUI.Button( new rect(x,y,width,height), string);
```

Note that the new rect class instance takes the x, y (position of the rect's upper-left corner) as well as the width and height dimensions of the button as the input.

Congratulations! By adding this line of code to the OnGUI() method, you will display a button at the x and y position with the text "string" on the button.

Detecting a mouse click

To detect a mouse click on this button, we need to check that the `GUI.Button()` function returns a Boolean; namely, `true` when the button is clicked and `false` otherwise. This means that every time the `OnGUI()` method is called, we have the opportunity to respond to a mouse click, each time a button is potentially drawn to the screen:

```
if (GUI.Button( new rect(x,y,width,height), string))
{
    // handle button click here
}
```

Building the main menu pop up

Let's put all of this together and build a functional and extensible pop up for the main menu.

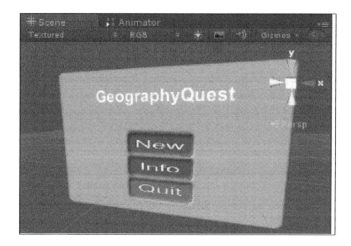

This pop up will display the name of the game on the title screen and present the user with three working buttons. From this, we will be able to make a pop-up Prefab that can be used for other UI. Perform the following steps to create a main menu pop up:

1. To start, let's create the base of the panel. Create a plane that will be the base of the pop up. Set its position to `0, 0, 8.6` and its X rotation to `-90`.

2. Scale the panel to `1.54, 1, 1` so that it is a bit wider than it is tall.

3. On the `MeshRenderer`, we associate a new material called `popupMaterial`. This material has a white-colored component and a texture that is opaque gray with round edges with full alpha. Applying this material makes the plane appear rounded at the corners.

4. Let's rename the plane to `popup_MainMenu` to reflect its actual role.

5. The main menu pop up will have four child objects: a text field for the pop-up title and three child objects for the buttons.

6. Create a `3DText` object, parent it to the `MainMenu` panel, and set its local position to `0`, `0.1`, `3`. This will place the text in front of the panel, that is, front and center. Set the anchor to `middleCenter` and the font size to `21`. Set the font style to `Bold`.

7. Move the game object to `-1.8,0.9,1.2` and scale down the font size to `15` to place and scale the text appropriately.

8. Let's create a button object to use the three interactive elements on the menu. To start, create a plane, rotate it by `-90` in the x plane, parent it to the `MainMenu` plane, and set its local position to `0,0.1,0.2`.

9. Set the scale of this new object to `0.3,0.1,0.2`. Rename it to `Button1` to make the object hierarchy more clear.

10. Create a `3DText` object, attach it to the button, and set the font size to `68`. Set the text field to `New`.

11. The first button will be for the new action. To handle this, we will need to write a script. Create a new script called `popupButtonScript.cs`. Attach an instance of this script to `Button1` (the new button).

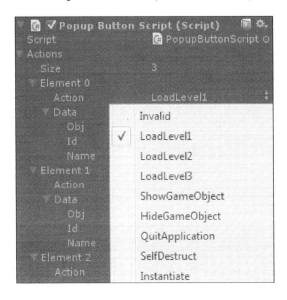

12. Inside this script, we will create a public enumeration that specifies all of the actions that can occur when the button is pressed. Loading levels one through three, showing and hiding GameObjects, instantiating a Prefab, self-destructing, and quitting the application will be the first actions our button supports:

```
public enum popUpAction {
  Invalid = -1,  //used to encode error action
  LoadLevel1 = 0,  //used to load level 0
  LoadLevel2 = 1,  //used to load level1
  LoadLevel3 = 2,  // used to load level2
  ShowGameObject =3,  //used to show a GameObject
  HideGameObject = 4,  //used to hide a GameObject
  QuitApplication = 5,  //used to quit application
  DestroyGameObject = 6, //used to destroy a GameObject instance
  Instantiate = 7 //used to instantiate an object from a prefab
}
```

13. We want to be able to set in script, when we click on a button, which action will be invoked on the click. This will require setting the enumeration as well as some side data that will be processed with the click. This class will be called popupResponse. In order to populate the array of actions on the button with this custom class, we need to make it serializable. Recall that if this class had inherited from MonoBehavior, then this would have included the serializable functionality; since we don't inherit from any base class, we need to add this back explicitly. This will allow the class properties to be saved inside the editor:

```
[System.Serializable]
public class popupResponse
{
  public popupAction action;
  public popupData data;
}
```

14. We will also need a class to describe the side data that the button needs to operate on when clicked. This will be contained in the serializable popupData class. This class contains a set of variables of different datatypes that a button may or may not use as side data while processing its action:

```
[System.Serializable]
public class popupData
{
  public GameObject obj; // a potential GameObject to operate on
  public int id; //an integer id to use when processing a popup
  public string name;//a string to use when processing a popup
}
```

15. We keep a list of actions (pop-up response classes) that will be invoked on a click on each button. This is kept as an array and not as a single response so that a button can perform an arbitrary number of tasks on a click.

```
public list<popupResponse> actions;
```

16. We create an enumeration for the current state of the button. This will be used to codify whether or not the mouse pointer is over the button and whether we should display the highlighted or non-highlighted texture:

```
public enum eButtonState
{
  Invalid = -1,
  Off = 0,
  On = 1 // a tri state enum used to encode if a button is clicked
  or not
};
```

17. We keep two variables of the `eButtonState` type. The `ButtonState` variable represents the current `eButtonState` of the button; namely, if it is `On` or `Off`. The `PrevTickButtonState` variable stores the `ButtonState` for every frame that the button itself updates. We use two state variables to search for the frame where the state changes so that we can dispatch the button actions on that frame:

```
Public eButtonState ButtonState;
Public eButtonSTate prevTickButtonState;
```

18. We add two public `Texture` references in this script. This allows the programmer to associate an `On` and `Off` texture for the button. When the mouse is over the button, the `On` texture will be displayed. When the mouse is not over the button, the `Off` texture will be shown:

```
Public Texture On;
Public Texture Off;
```

19. We keep references to the object named `Game` in the scene. We also keep a reference to the `gameManager` script attached to this. These are cached in the `start` method.

20. In the `Update()` loop of the button GameObject, we compare `prevTickButtonState` with `ButtonState`:

```
PrevTickButtonState = ButtonState;
```

21. In the `OnMouseDown()` method of this GameObject (mouse down on the button), we call the `Dispatch()` method, which iterates through all of the `buttonResponses` in the action list.

22. The `Dispatch()` method is where the brunt of the work for the button occurs. It loops over all of the actions in the action array (from `0` to `Count`):

```
for (int i= 0; I < actions.Count; i++)
{
  popupResponse r = actions[i];

}
```

23. A `switch` statement is used to selectively update the logic of the button based on the type of action in the actions array in each slot. Each potential `popupAction` has its own implementation in this block:

```
switch(r.action)
{
  // each case() implements a different behavior
}
```

24. The case for `LoadLevel 1`, `LoadLevel 2`, or `LoadLevel 3` will use the `GameMgr` component reference, and set the `GameState` in the `GameMgr` component to `levelLoad`, which then performs the `Application.LoadLevelAdditive` call.

25. The case for `Instantiate` will dereference the `GameObj` object in the `popupData sideData` member, and perform a `GameObject.Instantiate` call on it to duplicate that Prefab. It will then set the parent to the GameObject that has the name `'name'` from the **sideData** field. Lastly, it will set the position and orientation to `post` and rotation of the Prefab after it is initialized (the `pos` and `rot` values of the Prefab at the time it is created).

26. The `HideObject` and `ShowObject` actions will set the object referenced by the `sideData` to either `active =true` or `active=false`. This has the effect of disabling or enabling the renderer as well as the rest of the game logic/components on this object.

27. The self-destruct method will call `Destroy()` on the parent object of the button. This has the effect of destroying the pop up and all the children buttons and such. Of course, this assumes that buttons are a 1-layer child of the main pop-up root! Whether you decide to destroy or hide an object, it will depend on the specific needs of your game. Destroying an object will of course free up more memory; however, this should be done for every frame. If a lightweight way to hide and unhide an object is required, consider just disabling and enabling the renderer with `HideObject` and `ShowObject`.

Congratulations! We have an implemented popupButtonScript attached to our **NEW** button. Let's configure it:

1. On the **NEW** button, open up the popupButtonScript and set the number of actions to 2 (by manually setting size = 2). This will correspond to two actions that will be invoked, one at a time, on mouse click.

2. Set the action of **Element 0** to be LoadLevel1. Open up the **Data** field associated with this action and set the name to LEVEL1 (to match the scene file name).

3. For **Element 1**, set the action to SelfDestruct. By putting this second, we guarantee the button will load the new level and then destroy the pop up (which is what we want!).

4. Set the On texture to a light blue-colored texture and the Off texture to a dark blue variation. Set the ButtonState to Off by default.

Congratulations! We now have a working **NEW** button that starts a new game by loading a new level and destroying the menu pop up. At this point, we can delete the previous main menu page.

Let's continue building out the MainMenu Prefab:

1. Duplicate the **NEW** button twice, and translate the two copies below the first one to (0,0.1,-1.5) and (0,0.1,-3).

2. Rename the second button to Button2 and set the name of the text field to Info. Rename the third button to Button3 and set the name of the text field to QUIT.

3. Open the `popupButtonScript` on the third button, and change the `On` and `Off` textures to light and dark red textures, respectively. Change the number of actions in the script to `1` and set the action to `QuitApplication`.

4. Open the `popupButtonScript` on the second button and change two actions. The first one should be `Instantiate`, where `obj` is the `popup_Info` Prefab, and the parent object's name is codified under the name field `MainCamera`.

5. Set the second element of this array to `SelfDestruct`. With this, the **Info** button will create a new instance of a `popup_info` panel and destroy itself. The pattern we will use to return to the main menu will be such that the `popup_info` button allocates a new instance of the pop up when instructed to do so, after which it will destroy itself. In this way, the content of the UI pop up for both pages is completely contained inside the pop-up Prefabs we have created in the editor.

6. Let's create a new script that manages the pop up at its top level; call it `popupPanel`. Associate an instance of this script with the root of the `MainMenu`.

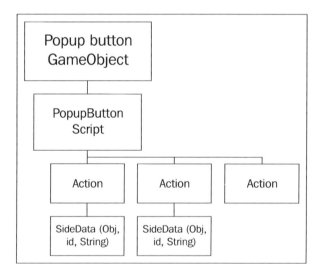

7. In this script, create a single public string named `nametxt` and a reference to `TextMesh`. In the `start` method, copy the public string variable's contents over the top of the string member of the `TextMesh`. This gives a simpler interface to name the pop up; we will use this script as a central place to interface with the pop up.

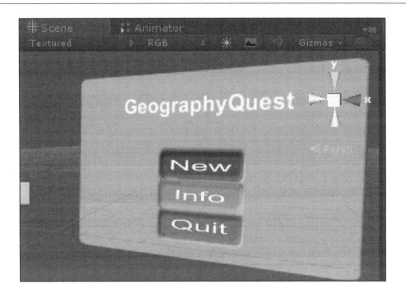

Great! Now, we have three functional buttons on our pop up. When we move over them, the `PopupButton` script swaps the highlighted and non-highlighted textures for an additional visual cue.

1. Drag-and-drop this pop up into the **Project** tab to make a Prefab out of it. Name the Prefab `popup_MainMenu`. We will need to reinstance our main menu from the Prefab at a later time.

2. Let's create a new Prefab based on this one. It will be used for the **Information** tab. To begin, copy and paste the `popup_MainMenu` Prefab. Rename it `popup_Info`.

3. Keeping the dimensions the same, rename the panel to `Info` by changing the pop-up name parameter in the `popupPanel` script.

4. Delete button 2 and button 3 from the `popup_Info` object; we only need one button on this panel to return to the main menu. Open the `popupButtonScript` on the single button and ensure that there are two valid actions.

5. Set the first action to `Instantiate`. In the data member for that action, set the `Obj` to instantiate to a reference to the `popup_MainMenu` Prefab. This will tell the button to create a copy of the `popup_MainMenu` Prefab when the button is clicked. To tell the script which GameObject to parent this new instance to, add the name of the object to the **Name** field and change the name field to `MainCamera`.

6. Set the second action to `SelfDestruct` so that this button will delete itself on a click.

7. In the `popup_Info` object, add five more `TextMesh` GameObject instances. Put them on successive lines at a distance of `0.8` units in z from one another. These will be used to store the lines of text in your information pop up. Set the first three lines of text to the following:

```
Geography Quest © 2014
PACKT Publishing
all rights reserved
```

8. Save this Prefab to the project folder by dragging-and-dropping it into your assets folder. Name the new Prefab `popup_Info`.

9. Go back to your `popup_MainMenu` and open up the button 2 `popupButtonScript` component. Find the `Instantiate` command in the actions array for this button. Now, go to the **Data** field for this action, and change the `obj` reference to the Prefab `popup_Info` by dragging-and-dropping it from the **Project** tab back to this field. Also, make sure the name of the parent object is also set at this time to `MainCamera`.

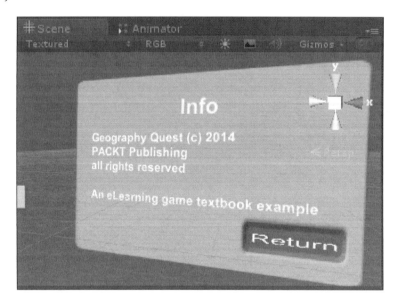

Congratulations! We now have a working information screen pop-up that has been connected to the **Info** button of our working main menu pop up. If you have not already done so, please delete the previous main menu panel from the last chapter; we will not need this anymore as our pop-up system can do the job of starting our game. Please make sure there is only one instance of `popup_MainMenu` attached to the camera by default, and that there is no `popup_info` object instance on the main camera by default.

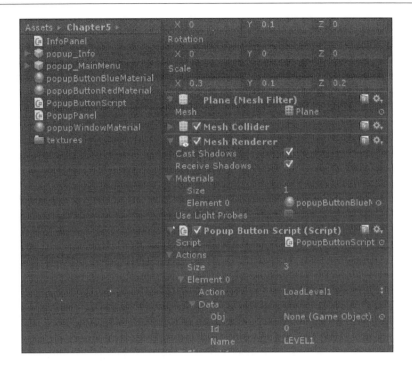

Testing our work

Let's trace through how the pop-up system works. When the main scene first loads, the popup_MainMenu Prefab renders in front of the camera. It does this because it is parented to the main camera's transform as a child object. This means that no matter what position and orientation the camera has, the pop up will move relative to this and always be on the screen, effectively in screen coordinates. This is a common trick in game programming used to achieve quasi-2D screen space results with 3D objects.

When the New button is clicked, the popupButtonScript iterates over the action array, and based on the enumeration for the action, it dispatches an appropriate command. For now, we set the GameState to loading level1 and let the gameManager script handle the loading of the new scene file. We then call SelfDestruct to delete the MainMenu object from the world (we won't need it anymore as we are in-game).

When the **Info** button is clicked, the popupButtonScript iterates over the action array, dispatching commands based on the value of the action enumeration. The first thing that happens is that popup_Info is instantiated and parented to the camera. Since this pop up has the same position and orientation as popup_MainMenu, the transition appears seamless! Then, popup_MainMenu is destroyed that leaves only the **Information** dialog displayed.

If the **Return** button on the popup_Info dialog is pressed, it iterates over its actions and invokes two commands. It instantiates popup_MainMenu again (from the Prefab in the **Project** window so that it is a new instance of the menu and not the original), then it calls selfDestructs and deletes the popup_Info window, leaving only the main menu. Since they share the same transform, the transition appears seamless.

If the **Quit** button is pressed, the application terminates. This is not readily apparent in the editor, but once we build to execute, this will terminate the program.

Future extensions

Now that we have a nice generic menu system, we could apply this to a number of situations:

- We can redesign our flag info pop up using a model similar to the popup_Info panel from the main menu. This would give each of them a **Return** button and a polished and consistent visual presentation.

- We can create a pause menu for the game. From this, the user can check statistics, restart the level, or quit to the main menu.

- We can use this system for NPC dialogs and interactions with the user. NPC dialogs are the conversation pop-up windows that will appear when the player interacts with NPCs. The user will interact with the NPC by selecting options from these pop-up windows.

Summary

We overviewed a wide variety of 2D and 3D user interface components that Unity provides. After some analysis, we determined the best scenarios to use each one of them. Finally, we applied our knowledge and built a pop-up system using programming techniques from previous chapters to build a generic, interactive, and responsive menu system. We built a couple of Prefabs and redesigned the frontend of the game using this new system to prove the efficiency of the technology. This adds a level of polish to our game.

In the next chapter, we will continue to add polish and interactivity as we program non-player characters for our game. By populating the game world with other characters and objects, it will add more depth to the game world that makes the experience more engaging, which will promote further learning by the user.

6
NPCs and Associated Technology

To increase the level of immersion in our e-learning game, we will want to increase the amount of user interaction scenarios. To do this, we will populate the game world with some non-player characters (otherwise known as NPCs) for the user to interact with. These are characters or actors in your game scene that the player can interact with during gameplay, but not control directly. You may find these referred to as AI Characters in other texts; however, these terms are synonymous.

In this chapter, we will build an NPC class to handle the choreography of these actors and their actions. To support the NPC system, we will develop a framework to define a smooth curve for the actors to travel on. We will also apply the FSM concepts from *Chapter 4*, *Mission One – Future Proofing the Code*, as we implement a data-driven behavior system; this will enable fast design and tweaking of NPC behavior inside the Unity Editor. Lastly, we will integrate these classes and construct Prefab objects to make the task of populating the world quick and simple.

The following topics will covered in this chapter:

- Creating the NPC GameObject
- Implementing the `SplineMgr` class
- Connecting `SplineMgr` to `npcScript`
- Implementing the NPC decision system
- Building a collection of NPC conditions and responses
- Putting it all together

Creating the NPC GameObject

To develop and test our NPC systems, we need a simple Prefab to represent our NPC character. Once this is working, we will be able to add polish to the game by replacing it with a more visually appealing model and by adding animation. To begin with, create a capsule with a scaled hat similar to the player Prefab placeholder.

Implementing the npcScript class

The npcScript class will encode the base state machine for NPCs. To develop a robust non-player character system requires a model of the behavior we want to present to the player. Once we have a model, we can build an FSM that meets our functional needs. We shall list these requirements in the following part.

In our e-learning game, the non-player characters will need to do the following:

- Travel about the world in a smooth, realistic way
- When approached by the player, the NPC should stop and face the player to interact
- When the player leaves the NPC or finishes the interaction, it should continue moving about the world

Based on these requirements, it is clear that we will need a number of states that we can encode in a public enumeration. To prove that the NPC framework works and meets our design needs, we will implement the patrol and turnToPlayer states as a minimum viable product for the NPC system. Once these are working, it will be clear that the system works and that the reader can then extend the system with more behaviors:

```
public enum npcState
{
   invalid = -1, //enum to encode error npc state
   none = 0,// enum to encode npc having no state
   idle = 1,// enum encoding npc waiting idly
   patrol = 2,// enum for npc patrolling about
   turnToPlayer = 3,// enum for npc to face player
   InteractWithPlayer = 4,// enum for npc interacting with player
   Celebrate = 5,// enum for npc celebrating
   Disappointed = 6 //enum for npc acting disappointed
};
```

Perform the following steps to implement the `npcScript` class:

1. A private variable of the type `npcState`, named `state`, will track the value of this enum for each NPC instance:

   ```
   private npcState state;
   ```

2. In order for our NPC to be able to follow a parametric curve when patrolling, we give the `npcScript` class a `SplineMgr` class to interpolate a user-defined path. A public `showPath` Boolean is also provided for debugging:

   ```
   public bool showPath;
   public SplineMgr path;
   ```

3. An instance of a data-driven system for detecting scenarios and dispatching responses at runtime is also added to the `npcScript` class. This class will act as the brain of the NPC, deciding when to change states based on the state of the game world:

   ```
   public npcDecisionMgr decisionMgr;
   ```

4. Each time an in-game NPC is activated, the `start()` script will first compute the debug path visualization for the spline and then set the NPC into the `patrol` mode so that it will start walking. The `computeDebugPath` method will walk through the spline from the start to the end and store a series of line segments that the debug line renderer can use to draw the spline when we need to visualize it. The second line of code sets the NPC into the `patrol` state, which tells the NPC to follow the spline path. We will discuss splines later in this chapter:

   ```
   path.computeDebugPath();
   SetState(npcState.patrol);
   ```

5. The `npcScript` class implements a `SetState(newstate s)` method to allow the client code to change the state of the NPC. A `switch` statement implementation provides a means of specializing one-off code that executes once when the state actually switches. This is how we implement the `OnEnter` event for each state in the enumeration.

6. When entering the `patrol` state, we set the head of the `SplineMgr` class to the NPC GameObject. This permits the `SplineMgr` class to attach the NPC to the curve and update its position each frame. We also set the playback mode on the `SplineMgr` class to loop so that when the NPC reaches the end of the curve, it will loop back to the start; other modes exhibit different playback behavior along the curve:

   ```
   path.HeadObj = this.gameObject;
   path.SetPlaybackMode(splineMgr.ePlaybackMode.loop);
   ```

7. When entering the `turnToPlayer` state, we set the playback mode of the `SplineMgr` class to none. This has the effect of stopping the velocity of the NPC model:

```
path.SetPlaybackMode (SplineMgr.ePlaybackMode.none);
```

8. The `npcScript` class implements an `Update()` method, (which all classes that inherit from `MonoBehavior` need to implement), which has four logical segments that are computed for each frame.

9. First, the distance from the player and the NPC is calculated. This quantity is stored for later processing:

```
if (player)
{
  Vector3 v = h.transform.position -
    this.transform.position;
  distanceToHero = v.magnitude;
}
```

10. A `switch` statement permits specialization of the code that the NPC needs to perform for each frame. In the `patrol` state, the NPC looks at the point in front of itself; this is a quantity that the `SplineMgr` class conveniently returns for us by evaluating the spline at a point slightly further ahead on the curve than the `HeadObj` itself:

```
this.transform.LookAt(path.TargetObj.transform.position);
```

11. While in the `turnToPlayer` state, the NPC looks at the player position:

```
this.transform.LookAt (player.transform.position);
```

12. If there is a `decisionMgr` class instance attached to the NPC, the `npcScript` allows it to evaluate all of its conditions for potential dispatch:

```
if (decisionMgr != null)
  decisionMgr.eval ();
```

13. Lastly, depending on the state of the `showPath` Boolean, we either enable or disable the `lineRenderer` component for the spline curve:

```
this.GetComponent<LineRenderer>().enabled = showPath;
```

Congratulations! You have just written the `npcScript` base framework for a non-player character class. As you can see, the power of this choreography class is derived from the FSM, and the work is delegated to the `DecisionMgr` and `SplineMgr` classes.

Implementing the SplineMgr class

Recall from our requirements that our NPC needs to be able to walk about the world along an arbitrary path. A convenient way to author the curve information would be by placing waypoints in the scene in the Unity3D Editor. Then, by interpolating between these points, we can apply smooth motion to the NPC object. It turns out that our `SplineMgr` is able to generate a curve that interpolates through all of the waypoints (or `ControlPoints`) in a set. Great news!

There are numerous types of splines in the mathematical world; each one has its own unique properties. Some of them don't interpolate any but get really close. Others will interpolate the first and the last, and approximate the middle two. By using a specific type of spline in our calculations (Catmull-Rom to be precise — named after the scientists who invented the formulation), we can guarantee that our curve will always interpolate all waypoints; the math inside our `GetPointOnCurve()` function returns a point on the Catmull-Rom spline curve.

We can implement the `SplineMgr` class using the following steps:

1. Our `SplineMgr` keeps a list of control points / waypoints for processing. These can be added to this list individually or in a batch via `splineNodeRoot` (this is simply an empty GameObject with a collection of control points in its hierarchy — a convenient way to encapsulate control point data).

2. The `SplineMgr` class has two types of playback. One of them evaluates the curve at a constant frame rate, and the other at a constant (more or less) arc length. The first way is good for curves that need to start and stop at a precise time. The tradeoff is that the curve may accelerate and decelerate as the control points move closer and farther away from one another.

3. The second playback mode is useful when the nature of the motion needs to be of constant velocity. However, the tradeoff with this playback type is that the total time to evaluate the curve is stretched:

```
public enum ePlaybackType
{
  invalid = -1,
  none = 0,
  const_dt = 1, //interpolate spline at constant speed
  const_dist = 2 //interpolate spline at constant distance steps
};
```

4. A single variable of the type `ePlayback` encodes the type of interpolation that the spline will use to generate points on the curve:

```
public ePlaybackType type = ePlaybackType.const_dt;
```

5. A second enumeration encodes the playback mode that the `SplineMgr` class will use to generate points on the curve. The loop will continue the playback in an infinite cycle. The `oneShot` mode will play the spline once and then finish. The `ComputingDebugPath` and `ComputingDebugPath_Finished` modes are used while evaluating the spline to generate points on the `lineRenderer` component:

```
public enum ePlaybackMode
{
  invalid = -1, //error spline interpolation
  none = 0, //not spline interpolation
  oneshot = 1, //play once and finish
  loop = 2, //loop continuously
  oneshot_finished = 4,//when  oneshot is done
  computingDebugPath = 5, //internal
  computingDebugPath_finished = 6 //internal
};
```

6. The `start()` method in the `SplineMgr` class performs two primary tasks:

   ○ It allocates a new GameObject to move along the curve in front of the `HeadObj` object. This is to facilitate looking ahead of the curve when the NPC is in the `patrol` mode and walking along the spline.

   ○ It also checks if a `splineNodeRoot` has been assigned to the spline. If it has, this triggers an automatic waypoint / control point installation into the `SplineMgr` class:

   ```
   TargetObj = new GameObject();
   nHead = 0;
   if (splineNodeRoot)
      InstallSplineNodes();
   ```

7. The `InstallSplineNodes()` method is an internal private method that takes a GameObject, extracts all child game objects, and then populates the `ControlPoints` list with these GameObjects as waypoints. The algorithm has three steps.

   1. First, the `ControlPoints` list is cleared:

   ```
   ControlPoints.Clear ();
   ```

   2. Using an internal function in Unity, we return an array of all the child objects of the `splineRootNode`:

   ```
   Transform[] allChildren = splineNodeRoot.GetComponentsInChil
   dren<Transform>();
   ```

3. We iterate over this list of child nodes (as they are the waypoints in our spline) and add them to the `ControlPoints` list. Note that this list will include the `splineNodeRoot`, so we need to check that we don't add this to the waypoints:

```
foreach (Transform child in allChildren)
{
  // do what you want with the transform
  if (child != splineNodeRoot.transform)
    ControlPoints.Add(child.gameObject);
}
```

8. The `ComputeDebugPath()` method iterates over the waypoints array before the game starts and fills in the `lineRenderer` component on the NPC. The `lineRenderer` component is then used to display the path if the `showPath` flag is set.

1. Before the method starts, it caches the playback mode and playback type that the user sets in the editor. We do this so that the system can set `playbackMode` to `ComputePath` while the `debugPath` is calculated:

```
// store settings
ePlaybackMode pbm = this.playbackMode;
ePlaybackType pbt = this.type;
```

2. We then loop over a preset number of samples in the `lineRenderer` component, sampling the `splinePath` and storing these samples in the `debugPath`:

```
SetPlaybackMode(splineMgr.ePlaybackMode.computingDebugPath);
for (int i = 0 ; i < 1024; i++)
{
  Vector3 p = getPointOnCurve();
  debugPath.SetPosition(i, p);
  if (IsFinished() == true)
  {
    debugPath.SetVertexCount(i-1);
    break;
  }
}
```

3. Once the path is calculated and the `lineRenderer` component is filled with values of line segments (from the `debugPath.SetPosition()` call earlier), we restore `playbackMode` and `playbacktype` from the user:

```
// restore values
playbackMode = pbm;
Playbacktype = pbt;
vOut = 0.5f * ((2.0f*p1) + (-p0+p2)*t + (2.0f*p0 - 5.0f*p1 +
4.0f*p2 - p3)*t2 + (-p0 + 3.0f*p1 - 3.0f*p2 + p3)*t3);
```

The `PointOnCurve()` method is the workhorse of the `SplineMgr` class. It takes four control points as input (p0, p1, p2, p3), and given a value of `t` from (0, 1), it returns a point on the curve. The polynomial equation in this function is derived from the Catmull-Rom spline basis matrix (other splines would have a different formula for computing a point on the curve; the important point is that our formula derived from that matrix).

9. In the `FixedUpdate()` method, we call a custom `eval()` method, which evaluates the spline. We call this during `FixedUpdate()` to simplify the `t` calculations in `PointOnCurve()`, eliminating the need to multiply by elapsed time. Had we decided to evaluate the spline during `Update()`, we would need to evaluate the curve on a point that was also a factor of the elapsed time:

```
// Update is called once per frame
void FixedUpdate ()
{
  if ((playbackMode != ePlaybackMode.computingDebugPath) &&
  (playbackMode != ePlaybackMode.none))
    eval ();
}
```

10. The `eval()` method is where the `SplineMgr` system evaluates the curve from being called every `FixedUpdate()`. Depending on the playback mode, it will either evaluate every frame or pause.

11. Recall that `SplineMgr` supports two playback types, `const_dt` and `const_distance`. In the `const_dt` mode, the spline is evaluated at `t+dt` every time `FixedUpdate()` is called:

```
if (type == ePlaybackType.const_dt)
  t += dt;
```

12. If the playback type is `const_dist`, the `SplineMgr` class will dynamically adjust the `dt` value for each frame so that the distance from the previous point on the curve to the next point on the curve is approximately equal to `target_arclength`. We use sequential search instead of binary search because it is less prone to getting stuck in high curvature segments.

13. Recall that a spline curve is defined over four control points. To build a longer curve composed of more points, we use a sliding window technique and construct tangent curves.

    Every frame, we update `t` by `dt` (or dynamic `dt`) and find a point on the curve for the relevant four control points. The four points that we pass into the spline evaluation method are the four points around the current moving windows view of the `ControlPoints` list:

```
// extract interpolated point from spline
//Vector3 vOut = new Vector3(0.0f, 0.0f, 0.0f);
vOut = Vector3.zero;
Vector3 p0 = ControlPoints[nHead].transform.position;
Vector3 p1 = ControlPoints[nHead+1].transform.position;
Vector3 p2 = ControlPoints[nHead+2].transform.position;
Vector3 p3 = ControlPoints[nHead+3].transform.position;
```

14. Once `t` exceeds `1.0`, this signals to slide `nHead` (the start of the window) up by `1`. Then, based on the playback mode, we either loop, stop, or handle the end of curve scenario in another appropriate way. Rather than setting `t` back to zero on a rollover, we subtract `1.0` instead. This way, we can capture the difference if `t` ever ends up slightly greater than `1.0` but less than `dt`; it happens more than you'd think, and doing this results in a smoother and more accurate curve:

```
if (t > 1.0f)
{
  t -= 1.0f;
  nHead++;
}
```

15. The `SplineMgr` class then translates the GameObject reference in `headObj` to the new position on the curve:

```
// update headObj
vOut = PointOnCurve(t, p0, p1, p2, p3);
if (HeadObj)
  HeadObj.transform.position = vOut;
```

16. The `SplineMgr` class also translates a second GameObject along the curve. The `TargetObj` object gets updated slightly in front of `headObj` and is used by the NPC to face forward when walking along the curve:

```
// update lookObj
if (TargetObj)
{
  Vector3 tgtPos = Vector3.zero;
  tgtPos = PointOnCurve (t+dt, p0, p1, p2, p3);
  TargetObj.transform.position = tgtPos;
}
```

Congratulations, we have now written a robust spline system for our NPCs and other moving objects! But how do we use it?

Connecting SplineMgr to NPCScript

To prepare a spline curve to be used by the `splineMgr` class, we can perform the following steps:

1. Create an empty GameObject, and set its position to (0,0,0). This will be the parent node to the collection of waypoints. Name it something appropriate, such as `curve1`.

2. Create a series of spheres named `waypoint1`, `waypoint2`, and so on. Note, we use GameObjects instead of empty objects so that we can enable the mesh renderer on the nodes if debugging or visualization is necessary. Our system will require a minimum of five points and two segments.

3. Arrange these points in the editor so that they form an appealing curve that meets your needs. Note that we interpolate the position of the waypoints only, so rotating them will not impact the trajectory of the interpolation.

4. Create a GameObject that will be used to interpolate the curve. Name it `SplineObj` and assign it to the `headObj` reference of the `SplineMgr` class.

5. Create a `lineRenderer` component, and attach it to the `headObj` object. Give the `lineRenderer` component 1024 position fields to start with so that it has enough pre-allocated segments to draw our curves.

6. Your curve should look something like the one in the following screenshot:

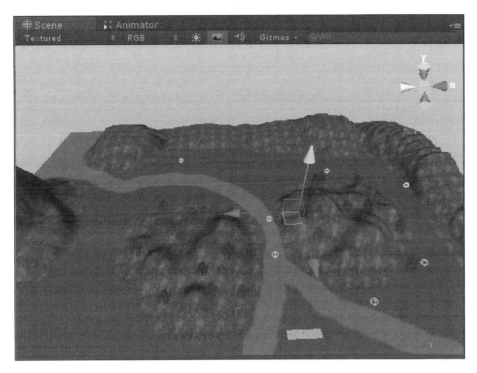

7. To playback the spline, create an instance of the SplineMgr class, and attach it to a GameObject. Set the dt variable and playback type to 0.1 and loop.

8. Assign curve1 to the SplineNodeRoot field of the splineMgr class.

9. Create an instance of npcScript, and attach it to the headObj object as well. Assign the SplineMgr component on the headObj object to the path reference in the npcScript class.

10. The DecisionMgr reference will remain empty for the time being. Not to worry! This just means that the NPC will have no way to change its internal state or react to the player. We will develop this system in the subsequent segment.

11. Once you have this system working, feel free to create another curve and another NPC to follow it. By following the same pattern, you can populate your game right away with simple moving objects.

12. Note that by switching from the `const_dt` playback to the `const_dist` playback, you can get a curve that either moves at a constant speed or finishes in a predictable amount of time. The first is useful for character motion, while the latter is for projectiles, animated objects, and other gameplay elements.

Congratulations! Your NPC can now walk along the path. Make sure you have selected the NPC in the editor to show the translation gizmo on the character while it moves; having a large frame of reference can help to debug the motion.

By ensuring that `showPath` is enabled on the NPC Script, your path should look as follows:

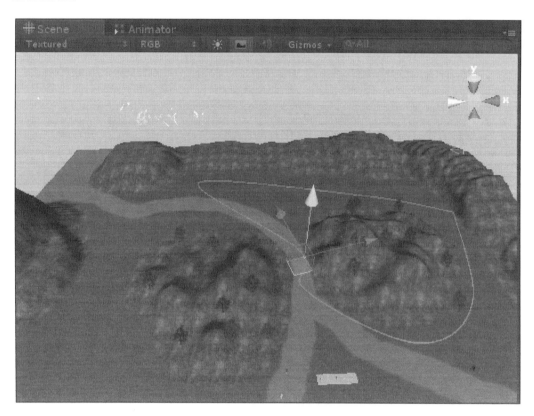

Implementing the NPC decision system

The NPCs in our e-learning game will need to be able to interact with the player and the world in addition to following a user-defined path. While the path-following code was easily encapsulated in one file, we will see that a general purpose solution to the first problem requires a more intricate design.

Our solution will be modeled around and function similarly to a question-and-answer system. A number of classes will be required for implementation:

- `npcCondition`: This is the base class for a question that the NPCs logic will ask about the player or the world.
- `npcResponse`: This is the base class for a response that the NPCs logic will invoke if a condition is found to be true.
- `npcInteraction`: This container class will house the association of a condition with a response. It will be responsible for testing if the condition is true (whatever the condition may be) and for invoking the appropriate response when that happens.
- `npcDecisionMgr`: This class is the brain of the NPC. It will house a collection of interactions and will ask these interactions to evaluate themselves. Since each interaction responds to the state of the world individually, the brain only needs to delegate this responsibility to each interaction! Simple, right?

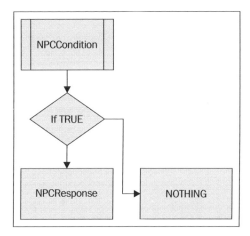

To prove that our `DecisionMgr` system works, we will need a few more specialization helper classes. These will help us see the system in action and validate its behavior.

- `condition_closerThanThresh`: This is a condition script that checks if the distance from object A to object B is less than a parameter. If it is, it returns true.

- `condition_fartherThanThresh`: This is a condition script that checks if the distance from object A to object B is greater than a parameter. If it is, it returns true.

- `response_changeState`: This is a response script that changes the state of an NPC to the state parameter.

Implementing the npcCondition script

The `npcCondition` class is the base class for all questions that an NPC might ask about the player or the state of the world.

1. Create a new class in the editor using the new class wizard. Name it `npcCondition`.

2. Open the script in MonoDevelop, and change the class declaration. Add the word `abstract` in front of `public` so that it reads the following. We use the keyword `abstract` because this class will be used to just declare an interface. We will use this class as a common base for all of the condition classes our game will have for NPCs:

   ```
   abstract public class npcCondition : MonoBehaviour{
   ```

3. Using the `abstract` keyword, declare an interface method named `eval()` with the following syntax:

   ```
   abstract public bool eval();
   ```

4. By designing `npcCondition` as an interface class, we are telling Unity that there will be a base class named `npcCondition`. Other conditions will be added to the game, and they will have different behaviors for sure, but one common element is that they all have a method named `eval()`, which they all implement in a unique way. In this way, each condition class can specialize its behavior through the `eval()` method, and no matter what is being evaluated, by returning `true`, we can pass a message to the `DecisionMgr` class that a condition has become true and that we need to invoke a response script.

In this way, we will need only to call `eval()` on `npcCondition` in the code, without the need to know specifically the type of condition being evaluated. This simplifies our code complexity immensely, allowing our condition code to be polymorphic, which is a good thing!

Implementing the npcResponse script

The npcResponse class is the base class for all responses that an NPC might invoke when a condition is found to be true.

1. Create a new class in the editor using the new class wizard. Name it npcResponse.

2. As seen previously, open the script in MonoDevelop, and change the class declaration; add the world abstract in front of the public so that it reads the following:

   ```
   abstract public class npcResponse : MonoBehaviour{
   ```

3. Using the abstract keyword, declare an interface method named dispatch() with the following syntax:

   ```
   abstract public bool dispatch();
   ```

4. As seen previously, by designing npcResponse as an interface class, we are telling Unity that there will be a base class named npcResponse. Other responses will be added to the game, and they will have different behaviors for sure, but one common element is that they all have a method named dispatch(), which they all implement in a unique way.

In this way, we will need only to call dispatch() on npcResponse in the code, without the need to know specifically the implementation of response that is being dispatched. This simplifies our code complexity immensely and allows our response code to be polymorphic as with the conditions.

Implementing the npcInteraction script

The npcInteraction class forms an association between a condition and a response; it is in fact a container for both a condition to test and a response to invoke if the condition is true. Remember, it could be any specific condition or response since those two classes are interfaces.

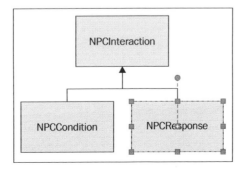

Perform the following steps to implement the `npcInteraction` script:

1. Create a new class in the editor. Name it `npcInteraction`.

2. Unlike the `npcCondition`, `npcReponse` classes, and most other classes to date, we will not derive this class from `MonoBehaviour`. Inheriting from `MonoBehaviour` is useful when you want to place your script onto a GameObject, and in most cases this is desired. For this script, we will not want to do that (you will see why in a moment). So remove the `MonoBehavior` line from the class declaration, and add the `[System.Serializable]` tag so that it resembles the following:

```
[System.Serializable]
public class npcInteraction {
```

   Adding the `Serializable` attribute is necessary when we don't inherit from `MonoBehaviour` because serialization is one of many features that `MonoBehaviour` provides to the child classes. We explicitly tag this class as serializable because we want to be able to save the instances of our class data in the editor. The difference here is that this script will not be attachable as a component on a GameObject but rather will appear in place in other classes as a member variable.

3. Add a public reference to `npcCondition` and `npcResponse`. Whenever this condition evaluates to `true`, the interaction class will dispatch the response:

```
public npcCondition condition;
public npcResponse response;
```

4. We also add an activated Boolean to allow us to selectively enable and disable interactions based on the state of the game:

```
public bool active;
```

5. The method `eval()` is where the brunt of the work in the interaction class is performed. It first checks if the interaction is active. If it is, and if there is a condition, it will evaluate the condition and check if that condition is true or not:

```
if (active == true)
{
  if (condition != null)
  {
    if (condition.eval() == true)
    { ...
```

6. Recall that the `npcCondition` reference could be any specialization of `npcCondition` so that the implementation of the `eval()` function could appear in any child class as long as it has been assigned in the inspector.

7. If the condition returns `true`, we check if a response class has been associated in the inspector. If it has been dispatched, we dispatch the response!

```
if (response != null)
    rval = response.dispatch();
```

Congratulations! We have implemented a container class that associates a generic condition with a generic response. We use the abstract keyword in the base class so that child classes that derive from `npcCondition` and `npcResponse` can all freely be connected to `npcInteraction`. Now let's look at how to connect our interactions together.

Implementing the npcDecisionMgr script

This class is the brain of the NPC. It contains a collection of the interactions that are constantly evaluated. If any condition is determined to be `true`, the appropriate response is dispatched. To construct it, we need to perform the following steps:

1. Create a new script named `npcDecisionMgr`.

2. As with `npcInteraction`, edit the class declaration to remove the inheritance from `MonoBehaviour`, and add explicit serialization so that the class data can be saved in the editor:

```
[System.Serializable]
public class npcDecisionMgr{
```

3. A public list of `npcInteraction` is exposed to the inspector. In here, a collection of condition/response pairs can be added for later evaluation. In this way, a whole set of logical interactions can be added to a character—all from within the editor!

```
public List<NpcInteraction> interactions;
```

4. The `eval()` method is used to visit each NPC interaction in the list, where each one is evaluated in turn; recall this checks the `condition.eval()` method for the condition member of the interaction:

```
foreach (npcInteraction e in interactions)
{
    e.eval();
}
```

Congratulations! You have completed writing the `DecisionMgr` class for the NPC. This is the class that will contain all of the logic for the NPC—what it will query in the world, and how it will respond to those queries.

Building a collection of NPC conditions and responses

To specialize how the NPC will respond, we need to write specific conditions and response classes and then populate the `DecisionMgr` for the NPC by placing these components in the editor. To prove this, let's develop a test case for an NPC that will perform the following logic:

1. Patrol on a curve, facing forward.
2. When the NPC gets close enough to the player, stop and face the player.
3. When the NPC is far enough away from the player, follow the path and face forward.

To implement this logic, we will need two conditions and one response.

Implementing the condition_ closerThanThresh script

Let's create a condition to check if the NPC is close enough to the player. This will be used by the `npcDecisionMgr` to determine when to stop patrolling and face the player.

1. Create a new script called `condition_closerThanthresh`.
2. In MonoDevelop, edit the signature of the class declaration so that it inherits from `npcCondition` rather than `MonoBehaviour`. Also, add the explicit serialization tag to this class so the editor can save it:

    ```
    [System.Serializable]
    public class condition_closerThanThresh : npcCondition {
    ```

3. This class will need three parameters to perform its tasks. A float to represent the target threshold, and two GameObject references for the two objects whose distance we will check:

    ```
    public float thresh;
    public GameObject trackObj;
    public GameObject baseObj;
    ```

4. We want to provide an implementation for the `eval()` method that was declared in the NPC base. To do this, note the syntax `public override bool`, which is as follows:

```
public override bool eval()
```

5. The `eval()` method will check the distance between the two GameObjects `trackObj` and `baseObj` for each frame. Don't forget these need to be set in the inspector; they can be the NPCs and the player or any two GameObjects for that matter (objects that have a transform):

```
bool rval = false;
Vector3 vDisp = (this.baseObj.transform.position -trackObj.
transform.position);
float dist = vDisp.magnitude;
if ( dist < thresh)
  rval = true;
return rval;
```

Congratulations, you have written a condition script that tests whether two GameObjects are closer than a set threshold.

Implementing the condition_fartherThanThresh script

Let's create a condition to check if the NPC is far enough from the player.

1. Create a new script called `condition_fartherThanthresh`.

2. In MonoDevelop, edit the signature of the class declaration so that it inherits from `npcCondition` rather than `MonoBehaviour`. Also add the explicit serialization tag to this class so the editor can save it:

```
[System.Serializable]
public class condition_fartherThanThresh : npcCondition {
```

3. The `eval()` method will have the same signature and implementation as the closer condition script explained previously, except that instead of checking if the distance is less than the threshold, you will check if the distance is greater than the threshold:

```
bool rval = false;
Vector3 vDisp = (this.baseObj.transform.position - trackObj.
transform.position);
float dist = vDisp.magnitude;
if ( dist > thresh)
  rval = true;
return rval;
```

Congratulations! You have combined the complement-condition script with the closer-than script. With both of these combined, we will be able to make the NPC start and stop a behavior based on proximity.

We need one more script to make the NPC respond to these proximity changes. Since the NPC knows how to behave in the `patrol` and `turnToPlayer` states, we want to make the NPC change the internal state as a response.

Implementing the response_changeState script

Let's create a response script that will change the internal state on the associated `npcScript` class to a specified value. This helper script will prove very useful as it will allow our NPC to react to conditions in the world by changing the `npcScript` state to response.

1. Create a new script in the editor, and name it `response_changeState`.

2. As with the previous two cases, modify the class signature to make it inherit from `npcResponse` (not `npcCondition`), and be sure to add the explicit serialization tag as well:

```
[System.Serializable]
public class response_changeState : npcResponse {
```

3. This class will have two members, an `npcState` enumeration and a reference to the `npcScript` class. When fired, the script will set the state on the `npcScript` reference to the value set in the local enumeration:

```
public npcScript.npcState newstate;
public npcScript npc;
```

4. As with classes that derive from `npcCondition`, we need to override the abstract method provided in the base class. Instead of `eval()`, we will override `dispatch()`:

```
public override bool dispatch()
```

5. If this response class has an NPC reference, it will set the value of `newState` on to NPC through the `SetState()` setter method that `npcScript` implements:

```
if (npc != null)
{
  npc.SetState (newstate);
  rval = true;
}
return rval;
```

Congratulations! We now have all the pieces to finally develop an `npcDecisionMgr` class that can tell the NPC to patrol or face the play when close enough. While it's true that we invest resources into developing a generic decision handling system, let's see how this pays dividends when implementing the logic in the editor.

Putting it all together

Let's test our `DecisionMgr` class by integrating these custom conditions and responses into an NPC instance.

1. Find the NPC instance from earlier, and select the `npcScript` class.

2. Note that the `DecisonMgr` reference is embedded in the class (instead of waiting for a reference to the GameObject). Click on the triangle, and notice that you can see the public interactions list that this class contains. By setting the size member variable, we can design and tailor the interactions for this NPC's `DecisionMgr` to perfectly match our gameplay needs.

3. Click on the size field of the interactions list, and set it to 2. We will have two interactions on this NPC.

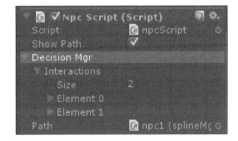

4. Click on the **Element 0** field. Make sure its active checkbox is set to `true`; this ensures that this interaction is always evaluated. Note that the **Condition** and **Response** fields are waiting for a reference to be set.

5. Drag-and-drop an instance of `condition_closerthanThresh`, and add it to the NPC.

6. Set the `thresh` to `15` units, the `trackObj` to the `npc`, and the `baseObj` to `Player`.

7. Drag-and-drop this component from the NPC into the condition field of interaction of **Element 0**. This associates this condition with the required interaction code. Note that if we forget to add the component to the `DecisionMgr` as we have done, the condition component will never get evaluated.

8. Drag-and-drop an instance of `response_changeState`, and add it to the NPC.

9. Set the NPC reference to the NPC that owns the component, and set the new state to `turnToPlayer`.

10. Drag-and-drop this component from the NPC into the response field of the interaction of **Element 0**. This associates the response with the required interaction code.

11. Drag-and-drop an instance of `condition_fartherThanThresh`, and add it to the NPC.

12. Set the `thresh` to `20` units, `trackObj` to the `npc`, and `baseObj` to `Player`.

13. Drag-and-drop this component from the NPC into the condition field of the **Interaction** tab of **Element 1**. This associates this condition with the second interactions code.

14. Drag-and drop-another instance of `response_setState` onto the NPC. Set the NPC to the parent NPC and the state to `patrol`.

Congratulations, we have configured the NPC `DecisionMgr` component to stop when it is close enough and turn to face the player. When the player leaves, the NPC will continue on its way. Adding further interactions to the NPC is as simple as increasing the size of the interactions array and creating the references.

Programming new interactions is a cinch, too! So long as we inherit from the correct base class, we see that gameplay code programming is now reduced to developing a library of query and interface classes. We no longer need to deal with the interactions and sequencing of logic, just the concrete behaviors themselves. This is a big win!

Summary

We developed a data-driven dispatch system of condition and response classes. We extended these bases to build a library of behaviors from which we can construct NPC behaviors. We then developed a decision-manage class that can evaluate these conditions and dispatch responses. This extendible pipeline can be specialized and quickly iterated upon in the Unity3D Editor. In the next chapter, we will put this to good use as we write the second level of our e-learning game. This level will take the knowledge learned from *Chapter 1, Introduction to E-Learning and the Three Cs of 3D Games*, and will test the player's recall in a fun and engaging way.

7
Mission Two – Testing a Player's Learning

In this chapter, we will program the second mission for our e-learning game. The objective of this level will be to test the learning that occurred in the first flag-collecting level. The theme of the level will be a race against two other NPCs through a park, where the player will have to answer trivia questions from NPCs placed randomly along the path. The player will have to achieve 100 percent accuracy and be placed first in the race in order to advance to level three.

In this chapter, we will cover the following topics:

- Exploring the structure of mission two
- Defining the framework for mission two
- Adding a mission to the `missionMgr` script
- Extending the `GameCam` script
- Modifying the terrain
- Adding NpcRacers to the mission
- Creating the start and finish line flags
- Creating the LevelStart and LevelFinished pop ups
- Creating the **setupLevel2** Prefab
- Creating the **raceStartup** Prefab
- Implementing the `LevelLogicObj` GameObject

Exploring the structure of mission two

The choice of a quiz race for mission two's gameplay was made to fill a number of e-learning game design requirements.

Recall that learning does not occur in a vacuum. Without testing for player comprehension, we cannot assess quantitatively how much learning has occurred, so a form of player interaction is necessary; the NPCs presenting the quiz cards fills this role. This is the source of challenge in the game.

The other racers chasing the player through the course add a level of pressure on the player. This is the source of intensity or pressure in the game.

Recall that testing and pressure are the two parameters necessary to create a learning environment that encourages cognitive flow. Having constructed our level according to this model, we can adjust the difficulty of the quiz questions and the speed of the other players to influence the fun and learning effectiveness of the game.

Defining the framework for mission two

As with mission one, we will organize our game objects into hierarchies as shown in the following screenshot:

The **_global** GameObject hierarchy will contain objects that persist for the entire lifespan of the game, and we will develop other hierarchies for objects that persist during a specific level.

To begin, let's create a new scene file for the level. Name the scene TESTBED2. Inside this scene, let's add two empty game objects at the root level, placed at (0,0,0) as with the first level. Name them **_global** and **_level2**.

1. Under **_global**, add the layer, camera, and GameObject. Recall that these objects and their scripts persist across all levels.

2. Under **_level2**, we will add level 2's specific GameObjects. As we create them throughout this chapter, we will add them to the hierarchy formed with the object named **_level2** as the root.

The following objects will be placed in this hierarchy:

- **_splineDataA** and **_splineDataB**: These are two collections of control points for the spline systems that racerA and racerB will use to follow smooth paths during the race.

- **GiantFlagFinish**: This is the large two-poled flag object representing the finish line.

- **LevelLogicObj**: This is the GameObject that contains the logic that will track the player's progress in the mission and dispatch either a success or failure condition based on this. This GameObject will also have a **GiantFlagStart** GameObject as a child, representing the starting line in the scene.

- **NpcLocators**: This is a collection of positions where NPCs will be randomly placed at the start of the mission. This operates similarly to the flag locators in mission one.

- **racerA**: This is an NPC GameObject that will race against the player.

- **racerB**: This is an NPC GameObject that will race against the player.

- **Terrain**: This is the terrain mesh that represents the park grounds in this level (mission two).

- **setupLevel2**: This is the GameObject instance that configures the level for play on start and starts the race.

- **raceStarter**: This is the GameObject instance that controls the start time of the race.

- **TriviaCards**: A number of trivia cards (one for each state) will be made that show the four flags to the player and ask him or her to pick the correct one for the given state name.

Adding a mission to the missionMgr script

Recall the `missionMgr` script attached to the GameObject (a child of **_global**). This is the class that manages tracking objectives in the game. In order to create a new mission for level two, let's perform the following steps:

1. Select the `missionMgr` script, and set the size of the mission's component to **1**, telling the system we will have one mission in this level.

2. Set the mission to **activated, visible,** and **MS_ACQUIRED** so that the level starting with this mission is ready to be processed from the start.

3. Set the display name to **win the race** and the description to **achieve 100% accuracy and first place in the race**.

4. Set the token component size to **0**. Another script will fill these dynamically, but eventually it will be filled with the randomly chosen flags from *Chapter 1, Introduction to E-Learning and the Three Cs of 3D Games*.

5. Set the points to **2500** and the reward object to **null**.

This is a sufficient setup for the mission on initialization.

Extending the GameCam script

The `GameCam` script's logic needs to be extended for this mission to support the ability to look up in the sky and back down at the player. To do this, a couple of simple methods need to be added to adjust the `lookat` GameObject.

A public method named `LookUp` will find the object named `lookUpTarget` and swap the `lookObj` in the script with the following code snippet:

```
public void LookUp()
{
    GameObject go = GameObject.Find("lookupTarget");
    if (go)
        lookObj = go;
}
```

 `lookUpTarget` is an empty GameObject parented to the player, placed 100 units above him or her in **Y** — a simple and effective way of looking up above the player.

A second method, named `LookPlayer`, will restore the `lookObj` back to the player object. This resets the camera back to third person functionality as shown in the following code snippet:

```
public void LookPlayer()
{
  if (trackObj)
    lookObj = trackObj;
}
```

Modifying the terrain

Since the theme of this level is a race, we need to create a nice winding path through the level. Select the terrain editor and paint a path from start to finish that loops around the mountains. At one end, we will place the racer, and at the end we will create a trigger to detect the end of the race, as you can see in the following screenshot:

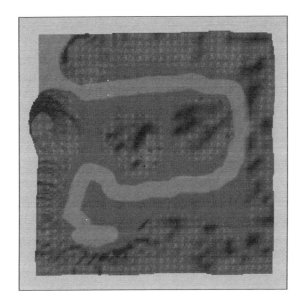

Adding NpcRacers to the mission

To make the race compelling and interesting, we will create two NPC racers to challenge the player. If it turns out well, we can build most of these with the technology we have already developed.

Each racer will need a spline to follow. Recall from the previous chapter that we developed a system for placing waypoints in the scene and using the `SplineMgr` script to generate a smooth curve for an NPC to follow. This will define the smooth path they traverse from start to finish. To implement the other racers in the level, carry out the following steps:

1. Create an empty GameObject, and name it **_splineDataA**. Create a series of sphere game objects, and place them in a path from start to finish. Disable the mesh renderer of these objects, and then parent them all to **_splineDataA**.

2. Create a second **_splineData** object with different path nodes so that the second racer will follow a similar but not identical route through the course. Name it **_splineDataB**.

3. Parent these two **_splineData** objects to the **_level2** root level object's container to ensure our level loading strategy remains simple and elegant.

4. As with the player, create a placeholder model for the racers, which is composed of a capsule with a rectangular hat parented to the top. Name them **RacerA** and **RacerB** respectively.

5. To **RacerA**, add an instance of `npcScript` (created in *Chapter 6, NPCs and Associated Technology*). Associate **_splineDataA** to the path reference on this script. Make sure the `DecisionMgr` member is empty; we won't be using it for the racers' logic. The structure of **RacerA** should then resemble the following figure:

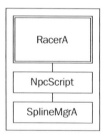

6. To **RacerA**, add an instance of the `SplineMgr` script. Set the **splineNodeRoot** to **_splineDataA** to install these control points into the manager class. Set the **playbackMode** to **paused** and the **playback type** to **const_dt** so that the `splineObject` starts stationary, but will move along the path with some natural looking acceleration and deceleration.

7. Follow steps 6 and 7 for **RacerB**, but associate **_splineDataB** instead of **_splineDataA**.

8. Set the speeds of racers (**dt** value) to **0.0015** and **0.001** respectively. This will set the racers' speeds to sufficiently similar values to make the race competitive.

9. Congratulations! You have implemented two racer NPCs that will compete with the player for first place in the race. Note that they don't have to wait to answer the quiz questions as the player does.

Creating the start and finish line flags

To mark the starting and ending location of the race, we will create a giant flag Prefab and instance it in both places. The banner of the flag will have cloth physics to give it an interesting motion. If you are targeting a lightweight device such as a phone, feel free to simply replace the cloth object with a flat plane if performance is an issue in your application. In order to create the start and finish line flags, we need to perform the following steps:

1. Create two cylindrical game objects. Set them three units apart from one another, and scale them up to a **y** value of **6**. Name these as **pole1** and **pole2**. In the scene view, you should see something like the following figure:

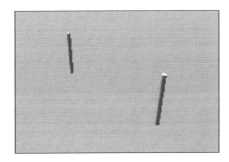

2. Create a cloth GameObject. It will appear as a flat plane in its initial position in the editor, but when you play the game, the cloth simulation will apply the motion.

3. Scale and rotate the cloth object so that it faces the ground at right angles. Scale the object so that it penetrates both poles. This will allow us to attach the cloth to the poles so that the physics simulation results in a draping banner.

4. Create an empty GameObject, and place it at ground level between the two poles. Name it **GiantFlag**.

5. Select the cloth object, and make sure the **Use Gravity** checkbox is selected.

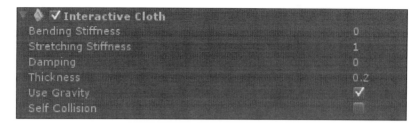

6. Select the **AttachedColliders** member of the cloth object. Set the size to **2**. Drag-and-drop the first pole into the first collider reference and the second pole into the second collider reference. This will bind the banner to both poles.

7. Create a material with a nice checkerboard material, and attach it to the cloth component.

8. Drag-and-drop this object to the project tab, and name the Prefab GiantFlag.

9. Create two instances of this **GiantFlag** Prefab—one at the starting line and one at the finish line of the path. Your flag should look something like the following screenshot:

Congratulations, you have created two banners for the game to mark the start and finish lines of the race! Click on the cloth simulation component of the **GiantFlag** Prefab, and experiment with the external acceleration, random acceleration, and friction variables to achieve different levels of motion in the banners themselves.

Creating the LevelStart and LevelFinished pop ups

Our level will use three pop-up windows to communicate with the start and finish scenarios of the level. One of them will show the start details, and the other one will explain whether you have passed or failed the objectives. We will use the Prefabs from *Chapter 5, User Interfaces in Unity*, as a basis for these pop ups. In order to create these pop ups, let's perform the following steps:

1. Create a new Prefab named **popup_Level2Start** from the **popup_info** Prefab, which we created in *Chapter 5, User Interfaces in Unity*.

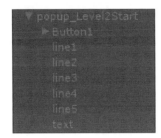

2. Change the five lines of text on the Prefab to detail the instructions for the level: "**You are in a trivia race against two other racers. Run from start to finish and answer the trivia questions. You must achieve 100 percent accuracy and place first in the race to move on to level 3. Good Luck.**".

3. On **Popup Button Script**, add three actions in the editor as shown in the following screenshot:

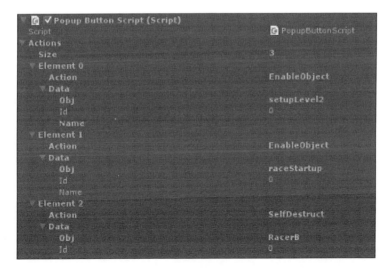

- ° On the first element of the actions array, set the action to **EnableObject** and the object reference to **setupLevel2** (a new GameObject parented to **_level2**). This object will set up the mission once it is instantiated.

- ° On the second element of the actions array, set the action to **EnableObject** and the object reference to **raceStarter** (a new GameObject parented to **_level2**). This object will commence the start-up of the racers themselves, resulting in their starting to run.

- ° On the third element of the actions array, add a **SelfDestruct** action so that the last task the button does is to destroy the panel itself.

4. Create a new Prefab named **popup_Level2Finish** from the **popup_info** Prefab, which we created in *Chapter 5, User Interfaces in Unity*.

5. Change the five lines of text on the Prefab to present a nice message to the user for winning the game. This panel will be enabled when the user wins the race with 100 percent accuracy.

6. Give the **confirm** button two actions: **LoadLevel3** and **SelfDestruct**. This will result in the button loading the next level and then destroying itself. In *Chapter 10, An Extensible Game Framework Pattern in Unity*, we will connect this pop-up window to the GameMgr class when we integrate the level transitions together.

7. Create a new Prefab named **popup_Level2Repeat** from the **popup_info** Prefab, which we created in *Chapter 5, User Interfaces in Unity*.

8. Change the five lines of text on the Prefab to present a message to the user for not winning the game. This panel will be enabled when the user doesn't win.

9. Give the **confirm** button two actions: **LoadLevel2** and **SelfDestruct**. **LoadLevel2** will have the effect of reloading the level once we integrate the level transitions together.

10. Set the **popup_Level2Repeat** and **popup_Level2Finish** pop ups to **disabled** in the editor, and keep the **popup_Level2Start** pop up enabled when the level starts.

Congratulations! The pop-up communication system for this mission is complete. Let's implement the Prefab that initializes the mission on start.

Creating the setupLevel2 Prefab

The **setupLevel2** Prefab will be activated when the user presses the **start** button on **popup_Level2Start**. It will finish the initialization of the mission for the level in the `missionMgr` script. Let's perform the following steps to create the **setupLevel2** Prefab:

1. Create a new Prefab named **setupLevel2**. Duplicate the `SetupMissionOne` script from mission one, and rename the duplicate `SetupMissionTwo`. Add an instance to **setupLevel2**.

2. Inside MonoDevelop, change the class declaration to `SetupMissionTwo` as shown in the following line of code:

   ```
   public class SetupMissionTwo : MonoBehavior {
   ```

3. We will use the same pattern for choosing random `QuizNpc` locators as we did for the flag locators in mission one. In addition to the **QuizNpc** Prefabs and the **spawnPoints** lists, add a list of `CorrectPopups` to the class.

4. This class will hold the pop ups that are shown to the user when a correct answer is given for a particular quiz question. This will be populated by the user in the editor, and it will hold a number of unique pop ups, which will give the user a mission token when clicked through. We will store these unique pop ups in a list, as declared in the following line of code:

   ```
   public List<GameObject> CorrectPopups
   ```

5. Add a public reference to **QuizNpc** Prefab. This is the model (and eventually animations) for the `QuizNpc` class on the path giving the questions. Once the locations are randomly chosen, instances of this model will be placed around the track. This can be done with the following line of code:

   ```
   public GameObject QuizNpc;
   ```

6. We will also keep a reference to the `raceStarterObj` so that we can enable it when the `setupLevel2` class is enabled. This will have the effect of starting the racers' movement. This can be done with the following line of code:

   ```
   public GameObject RaceStarterObj;
   ```

   This script works largely in the same way as `SetupMissionOne`, with some subtle changes due to the different design needs. As five random quiz cards are selected (rather than flags), we instantiate `QuizNpc` to stand that location:

   ```
   GameObject QuizNpcInstance =
     (GameObject)Instantiate(QuizNpc, QuizPos, new
     Quaternion(0,0,0,1));
   ```

7. As we loop over the selected questions, we hand off the correct answer pop up for each NPC question to the `QuizNpc` class itself. The NPC will then hand this off when the quiz question is actually activated (when player is close enough to NPC). The NPC stores the reference to the correct answer pop up through a `QuizNpcHelper` script attached to it as shown in the following code snippet:

```
QuizNpcIstance.GetComponent<QuizNpcHelper>().SetPrefabRefer
    ence( CorrectPopups[k]);
QuizNpcInstance.SetActive(true);
```

8. We install the QuizCard itself into NPC's `ObjectInteraction` inside the Prefab member variable of the `setupLevel2` class. This allows `interactiveObject` to display the QuizCard when the player is close enough as shown in the following code snippet:

```
ObjectInteraction oo =
    QuizNpc.GetComponent<objectInteraction>();
if (oo)
    oo.prefab = quizPrefab;
```

9. Then we add `MissionToken` from the current chosen pop up and add it to `missionTokens` of the mission for this level. This way, the mission can track the randomly chosen quiz questions from this method as shown in the following code snippet:

```
mm.missions[0].tokens.Add(CorrectPopups[k].
    GetComponent<MissionToken>();
```

10. Congratulations! `SetupMissionTwo` is finished. When the **setupLevel2** Prefab is enabled (by clicking on **Okay** on **popup_Level2Start**), the `setupMissionTwo` script will choose five random quiz locations from a group of ten and five random quiz cards from a group of 50. It will then place instances of `quizNpc` at each location for the player to interact with.

Creating the raceStartup Prefab

Recall that the second Prefab that is enabled when the **popup_Level2Start** windows is clicked, is the **raceStartup** Prefab. This object will commence the start of the other racers, leaving room for an eventual countdown clock. Let's start creating the **raceStartup** Prefab by performing the following steps:

1. Create a new empty GameObject named `RaceStartup`.

2. Create a new script named `RaceStarterScript`, and add an instance of it to the `raceStartup` class.

3. This class should have a number of public variables to permit the tweaking of the race start.

4. In the following line of code, `stageTime` is the amount of time each stage lasts:

    ```
    public float stageTime = 2.0f;
    ```

5. In the following line of code, `numStates` is the number of states (of duration `stageTime`) that need to pass before the NPCs are activated:

    ```
    public int numStages = 4;
    ```

6. In the following line of code, `currentState` tracks which actual state is currently elapsing:

    ```
    public int currentState = 0;
    ```

7. Add a float `t` to track elapsed time as shown in the following line of code:

    ```
    public float t;
    ```

8. Add two GameObject references to NPCs to activate as shown in the following lines of code:

    ```
    public GameObject npcA;
    public GameObject npcB;
    ```

9. The core logic for this class happens in the `Update()` method each time Unity invokes this function and we track total elapsed time in `t` as shown in the following line of code:

    ```
    t += time.deltaTime;
    ```

10. Once the final state is completed, we tell each NPC to change state to `patrol`. This has the effect of making them start to follow their spline paths via their component `SplineMgrs` as shown in the following code snippet:

    ```
    if (currentState == numStates + 1)
    {
      ncpA.GetComponent<npcScript>().SetState(npcScript.npcState.
        patrol);

      npcB.GetComponent<npcScript>().SetState(npcScript.npcState.
        patrol);
    ```

11. If the elapsed time exceeds the state time, we reset the `stageTime` to zero plus any fractional difference beyond the `stageTime` that has been incurred and then increase the stage count by 1. This is slightly more accurate than simply setting `t` to `0` for each stage and is prone to fewer errors over many stages. This can be accomplished with the following code snippet:

```
if (t > stageTime)
{
    currentState++;
    t -= stageTime;
}
```

Congratulations! Now, the **raceStartup** Prefab will activate the NPCs after an appropriate time has passed. Conveniently, this delay is adjustable inside the Unity Editor. This is a good thing as it lets the player to get a small head start on the other racers.

Implementing the LevelLogicObj GameObject

When instantiated, the `LevelLogicObj` object will be detected as soon as the player and racers enter the LevellogicObj's trigger volume. When three racers have crossed the finish line, it will determine if the player has met the objectives of the race or not, and it will enable either the pass or fail retry pop up. In order to implement the `LevelLogicObj` object, we need to perform the following steps:

1. Create a cube game object named `LevelLogicObj`. Scale, orient, and position it so that it surrounds the finish line in the level as shown in the following screenshot:

2. Make sure it has a **Box Collider** component and that the **Is Trigger** checkbox is checked as shown in the following screenshot:

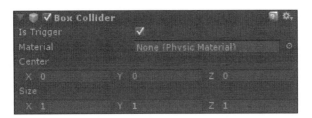

3. We want to use the `DecisionMgr` class to track the progress of the racers, which means we need to add an instance of `npcScript` to this object.

4. Don't worry about the fact that the `LevelLogicObj` object is not specifically an NPC; if an existing tool is appropriate, don't reinvent the wheel!

5. Create a new script called `listData`. Modify it so that it inherits from `npcCondition` (just as the rest of the conditions we have developed so far). Add a public list of GameObjects called `_ListData` as shown in the following line of code:

```
public List<GameObject> _ListData;
```

6. By inheriting from `npcCondition`, we now have a designer tweakable array that can be associated with `DecisionMgr` at runtime. Just don't forget to add the additional `using` directive for the list as shown in the following line of code:

```
using System.Collections.Generic;
```

7. Add an instance of `listData` to the `LevelLogicObj` object, and then drag-and-drop the script component into the first interaction's condition reference field.

8. The first logical operation that `LevelLogicObj` needs to do is, when a character or the player enters the `triggerVolume`, a reference to that GameObject should be stored in the data container. In our example, that container is `listData`. We need to implement a way to detect and insert. So, create a new script named `condition_OnEnter`, and add an instance of it to the `LevelLogicObj` object.

9. Modify the `condition_OnEnter` condition script so that it inherits from `npcCondition` rather than `monobehavior` as with the rest of our condition classes as shown in the following line of code:

```
public class condition_onEnter : npcCondition;
```

10. Give the `condition_OnEnter` class a public reference to a GameObject called `trackObj`. This will hold a reference to the most recent GameObject that enters the trigger volume. This can be done with the following line of code:

```
public GameObject trackObj;
```

11. Add a private Boolean variable named `hasEntered`, and initialize it to `false`. This will be used to track whether an object is actually inside the volume (rather than only having entered this frame):

```
private bool hasEntered = false;
```

12. Now recall that the `OnTriggerEnter`/`OnTriggerExit` callbacks are returned from the physics system rather than our DecisionMgr system. In order to interface the two, we will implement `OnTriggerEnter` and `OnTriggerExit` and then pass the relevant information outward.

13. The `OnTriggerEnter` method should simply set `hasEntered` to `true`, and it should set `trackObj` to `other.gameObject` as shown in the following code snippet:

```
void OnTriggerEnter(collider other)
{
   hasEntered = true;
   trackObj = other.gameObject;
}
```

14. The `OnTriggerEnter` method should conversely set `hasEntered` to `false`, and it should nullify `trackObj` as shown in the following code snippet:

```
void OnTriggerExit(Collider other)
{
   hasEntered = false;
   trackObj = null;
}
```

15. Lastly, the `eval()` method for this condition should be implemented to return the `hasEntered` variable. Recall from when we first developed the npcCondition system that the keyword override is used when declaring this `eval()` method to tell the Unity C# compiler that this implementation of the method corresponds to the interface declared in the `npcCondition` base class. In this way, we have now paired the PhysX trigger system with our DecisionMgr. When the **Is Trigger** checkbox fires the `OnTriggerEnter()` method even when the player or racer crosses the finish line, it will pass the reference from the GameObject that entered the trigger to this condition class. This can be accomplished with the following code snippet:

```
public override bool eval()
{
   return hasEntered;
}
```

16. Setting our attention on the response we need to write, let's create a new script named `response_insert` and add an instance of it to `LeveLLogicObj`.

17. Modify the script so that it inherits from `npcResponse` rather than `Monobehavior`. Don't forget to add the `[System.Serializable]` flag to the script.

18. Add a public `npcCondition` variable named data, as shown in the following line of code:

    ```
    public npcCondition data
    ```

19. At this point, we recognize that in our base `npcReponse` and `npcCondition` classes, we need to track the paired response or condition from the interaction. As such, go into these classes now, and add a public `conditionAssociation` to `npcResponse` and add a public `responseAssociation` to `npcCondition`.

20. Switching back to `response_Insert`, we start to implement the `dispatch()` method. We first get `condition_OnEnter()` associated with this response's interaction and check if the GameObject that actually entered is an NPC racer or the player. We determine this by checking the tag on the object that entered as shown in the following code snippet:

    ```
    condition_onEnter cOE = (conditionAssciation as
       condition_onEnter);
       bool bIsPlayer = (cOE).trackObj.CompareTag("Player");
       bool bIsRacer = (cOE).trackObj.CompareTag("Character");
    ```

21. If the object that entered is either a racer or player, insert the GameObject reference into the `listData` condition wrapper. For safety, we only insert a GameObject if it has not already been inserted into the list as shown in the following code snippet:

    ```
    listData rlist = (data as listData);
       if (!rlist._a.Contains(coe.trackObj))
         rlist._listData.Add(cOE.trackObj);
    ```

22. If a racer (not the player) entered the finish line, we set the racer to paused so that it doesn't keep traversing its `SplinePath` as shown in the following code snippet:

    ```
    (if bIsRacer)
    {
    (cOE).trackObj.GetComponent<npcScript>().SetState(npcScript
       .npcState.pause);
    ```

23. Now that `reponse_insert` has been implemented, drag-and-drop the `listData` script from the `LevelLogicObj` object to the data field on this script. Then, drag-and-drop the instance of this script from `LevelLogicObj` to the second response field of LevelLogicObj's DecisionMgr.

24. For the third condition, we need to create a new condition script called `condition_listFull`. Go ahead and make a new script; change its base class to `npcCondition` and add an instance to `LevelLogicObj` as usual.

25. Add a public variable to this script to track the number of entries that will represent `full`, and a public `npcCondition` called `data`, as shown in the following code snippet:

```
public int numEntries;
public npcCondition data;
```

26. Drag-and-drop `listData` from the `LevelLogicObj` GameObject to the data field on `condition_listFull`.

27. Inside the implementation of `eval()`, `condition_isFull` does its work. If data is not null, it extracts the number of entries from the listData's list through its count member as shown in the following code:

```
if (data != null)
{
    int count = (data as listData)._listData.Count;
```

28. If the count of the `listData` component's list array equals the `numEntries` value on this script, the return value is set to `true`. Otherwise, it remains `false` as shown in the following code snippet:

```
if (count == numEntries)
    rval = true;
```

29. Now that `condition_listFull` is complete, let's create the response that will occur when the list is found to be true — `response_ShowRaceResultsPopup`. This script will check the status of the mission, and enable the correct pop up on the main camera to achieve the desired gameflow.

30. Create a new script named `response_ShowRaceResultsPopup`, change its base class to `npcResponse`, and add an instance of it to `LevelLogicObj`.

31. Add the following five public member variables to this script:

    ○ An npcCondition named `data`

    ○ A GameObject named `player`

    ○ A gameMgr named `gm`

    ○ A GameObject named `passPopup`

    ○ A GameObject named `retryPopup`

The `response_ShowRaceResultsPopup` class will use the `GameManager` reference, and based on the data condition and result, it will enable either `passPopup` or `retryPopup`.

32. Edit `response_ShowRaceResultsPopup` so that its base is `npcResponse`.

33. Drag-and-drop the `listData` component from `LevelLogicObj` to the data field of this script.

34. Drag-and-drop the `GameMgr` script from the GameObject to the **Gm** field of this script. Recall that this GameObject lives as a child of the **_global** GameObject.

35. Drag-and-drop the `player1` reference from beneath **_global** to the player reference in this response script.

36. Drag-and-drop the **popup_Level2Finish** pop up from beneath **MainCamera** (which is beneath **_global**) to the **pass** reference field of this script.

37. Drag-and-drop the **popup_Level2Repeat** pop up from beneath **MainCamera** to the **fail** reference field of this script. At this point your component should look somewhat like the following screenshot:

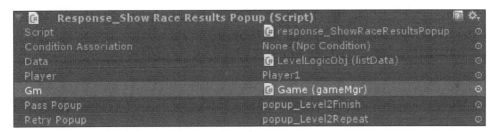

38. Inside this script, the `dispatch()` method does the brunt of the work. We compute if the player is first by checking if the `player` reference is equal to the first cell in the `listData` component's list array, as shown in the following code snippet:

```
bool playerIsFirst = (data as listData)._listData[0] ==
    player;
```

39. If the player is first, and we can locate the `missionMgr` script from the game, we point the camera looking up (to make sure the pop up is shown with a nice effect) as shown in the following code snippet:

```
if (mm)
    Camera.main.Getcomponent<GameCam>().LookUp();
```

40. We then check the `missionMgr` script for the status of the first mission. At this point, we know the game is done because the list is full, but the player may or may not have got 100 percent. If the player achieved 100 percent on the quiz, it means that the first mission is complete, and hence we should activate the pass pop up as shown in the following code snippet:

```
if (mm.isMissionComplete(0) == true)
{
    passPopup.SetActive(true);
}
```

41. Otherwise, we activate the fail pop up as shown in the following code snippet:

```
else
{
    fail.Popup.SetActive(true)
}
```

42. Excellent! At this point, `DecisionMgr` is fully populated and should look somewhat like the following screenshot:

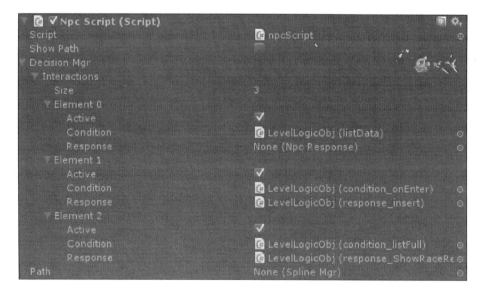

43. Congratulations! The `LevelLogicObj` evaluates the conditions of inserting a character during the `OnEnter()` method and of displaying the correct pop up when the list is full. We use `DecisionMgr` rather than the mission system to show how a pipeline can be built that allows complex game logic to be developed simply from parts that can be manipulated inside of Unity.

Summary

We have finished mission two in our e-learning game, which tests the user on the learning that occurred in mission one by developing a race-based quiz game. The elements of fun and pressure are deliberate design considerations as they allow the designer a way to adjust the fun factor of the game to enhance learning.

In the next chapter, we will change focus and learn about how to add models and animations to the placeholder characters and objects in our game in order to make them more visually appealing.

8
Adding Animations

Until this point, we have been successfully developing our game with the in-editor primitives provided by Unity3D. To add a professional layer of polish, we will learn how to add skinned models and various types of animations to our e-learning game. We will download skinned mesh models and animations from a popular site and learn how to integrate them into the game, as we develop a character motion system. We will also learn about the in-editor animation editor and how it can be used to animate static meshes (appropriate for in-game models such as buildings, cars, and statues that are not weighted to a 3D skeletal hierarchy).

In this chapter, we will discuss the following topics:

- Exploring 3D hierarchies
- Skinned meshes in Unity3D
- Exploring the Mechanim animation system
- Exploring the Unity Animation editor

Exploring 3D hierarchies

The ability to parent objects among one another is a versatile feature in Unity3D. So far, in this book, we have seen how hierarchies can be used as a means of associating objects with one another and organizing them into hierarchies. One example of this is the character Prefabs with their child hats we developed for the player Prefab and the racers. In this example, by dragging-and-dropping the hat object onto the player's body, we associated the hat with the object body by putting the child into the parent's coordinate system. After doing this, we saw that the rotations, translations, and scales of the body's transform component were propagated to the hat. In practice, this is how we attach objects to one another in 3D games, that is, by parenting them to different parents and thereby changing their coordinate systems or frames of reference.

Another example of using hierarchies as a data structure was for collections. Examples of this are the `splineData` collections we developed for the NPCs. These objects had a single game object at the head and a collection of data as child objects. We could then perform operations on the head, which lets us process all of the child objects in the collection (in our case, installing the way points).

A third use of hierarchies was for animation. Since rotations, translations, and scales that are applied to a parent transform are propagated to all of the children, we have a way of developing fine-tuned motion for a hierarchy of objects. It turns out that characters in games and animated objects alike use this *hierarchy of transforms* technique to implement their motion.

Skinned meshes in Unity3D

A skinned mesh is a set of polygons whose positions and rotations are computed based on the positions of the various transforms in a hierarchy. Instead of each GameObject in the hierarchy have its own mesh, a single set of polygons is shared across a number of transforms. This results in a single mesh that we call a skin because it envelops the transforms in a skin-like structure. It turns out that this type of mesh is great for in-game characters because it moves like skin.

 We will now use www.mixamo.com to download some free models and animations for our game.

Acquiring and importing models

Let's download a character model for the hero of our game.

1. Open your favorite Internet browser and go to www.mixamo.com.

2. Click on **Characters** and scroll through the list of skinned models. From the models that are listed free, choose the one that you want to use. At the time of writing this book, we chose **Justin** from the free models available, as shown in the following screenshot:

Justin

Free

3. Click on **Justin** and you will be presented with a preview window of the character on the next page. Click on **Download** to prepare the model for download. Note, you may have to sign up for an account on the website to continue.

4. Once you have clicked on **Download**, the small downloads pop-up window at the bottom-right corner of the screen will contain your model. Open the tab and select the model. Make sure to set the download format to **FBX for Unity (.fbx)** and then click on **Download** again. **FBX (Filmbox)**—originally created by a company of the same name and now owned by AutoDesk—is an industry standard format for models and animations. Congratulations! You have downloaded the model we will use for the main player character.

5. While this model will be downloaded and saved to the `Downloads` folder of your browser, go back to the character select page and choose two more models to use for other NPCs in the game. At the time of writing this book, we chose **Alexis** and **Zombie** from the selection of free models, as shown in the following screenshot:

6. Go to Unity, create a folder in your **Project** tab named `Chapter8`, and inside this folder, create a folder named `models`. Right-click on this folder and select **Open In Explorer**. Once you have the folder opened, drag-and-drop the two character models from your `Download` folder into the `models` folder. This will trigger the process of importing a model into Unity, and you should then see your models in your **Project** view as shown in the following screenshot:

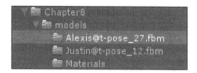

7. Click on each model in the `models` folder, and note that the **Preview** tab shows a t-pose of the model as well as some import options. In the **Inspector** pane, under the **Rig** tab, ensure that **Animation Type** is set to **Humanoid** instead of **Generic**. The various rig options tell Unity how to animate the skinned mesh on the model. While **Generic** would work, choosing **Humanoid** will give us more options when animating under Mechanim. Let Unity create the avatar definition file for you and you can simply click on **Apply** to change the **Rig** settings, as shown in the following screenshot:

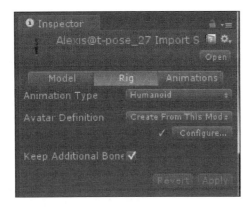

8.   We can now drag-and-drop your characters to the game from the **Project** tab into the **Scene** view of the level, as shown in the following screenshot:

Congratulations! You have successfully downloaded, imported, and instantiated skinned mesh models. Now, let's learn how to animate them, and we will do this starting with the main player's character.

Exploring the Mechanim animation system

The Mechanim animation system allows the Unity3D user to integrate animations into complex state machines in an intuitive and visual way! It also has advanced features that allow the user to fine-tune the motion of their characters, right from the use of blend trees to mix, combine, and switch between animations as well as **Inverse Kinematics (IK)** to adjust the hands and feet of the character after animating. To develop an FSM for our main player, we need to consider the gameplay, moves, and features that the player represents in the game.

Choosing appropriate animations

In level one, our character needs to be able to walk around the world collecting flags and returning them to the flag monument. Let's go back to www.mixamo.com, click on **Animations**, and download the free **Idle**, **Gangnam Style**, and **Zombie Running** animations, as shown in the following screenshot:

Building a simple character animation FSM

Let's build an FSM that the main character will use. To start, let's develop the locomotion system.

1. Import the downloaded animations to a new folder named anims, in Chapter8. If you downloaded the animations attached to a skin, don't worry. We can remove it from the model, when it is imported, and apply it to the animation FSM that you will build.

2. Open the scene file from the first gameplay level TESTBED1.

3. Drag-and-drop the **Justin** model from the **Projects** tab into the **Scene** view and rename it **Justin**.

4. Click on **Justin** and add an **Animator** component. This is the component that drives a character with the Mechanim system. Once you have added this component, you will be able to animate the character with the Mechanim system.

5. Create a new animator controller and call it JustinController.

6. Drag-and-drop JustinController into the controller reference on the **Animator** component of the Justin instance. The animator controller is the file that will store the specific Mechanim FSM that the **Animator** component will use to drive the character. Think of it as a container for the FSM.

7. Click on the `Justin@t-pose` model from the **Project** tab, and drag-and-drop the avatar definition file from **Model** to the **Avatar** reference on the **Animator** component on the **Justin** instance.

8. Go to the **Window** drop-down menu and select **Animator**. You will see a new tab open up beside the **Scene** view. With your **Justin** model selected, you should see an empty **Animator** panel inside the tab, as shown in the following screenshot:

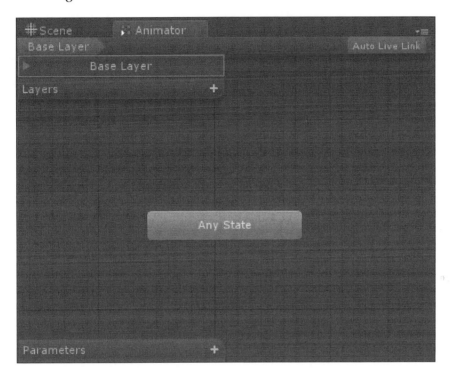

9. Right now our **Justin** model has no animations in his FSM. Let's add the idle animation (named `Idle_1`) from the **Adam** model we downloaded. You can drag-and-drop it from the **Project** view to any location inside this panel.

   That's all there is to it! Now, we have a single `anim` FSM attached to our character. When you play the game now, it should show **Justin** playing the `Idle` animation. You may notice that the loop doesn't repeat or cycle repeatedly. To fix this, you need to duplicate the animation and then select the **Loop Pose** checkbox.

10. Highlight the animation child object `idle_1` and press the *Ctrl + D* shortcut to duplicate it. The duplicate will appear outside of the hierarchy. You can then rename it to a name of your choice. Let's choose `Idle` as shown in the following screenshot:

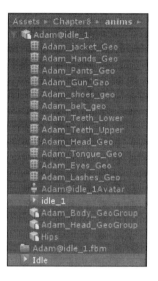

11. Now, click on `Idle`, and in the **Inspector** window, make sure that **Loop Pose** is selected.

Congratulations! Using this `Idle` animation now results in a character who idles in a loop. Let's take a look at adding the walk animation.

12. Click on the **Zombie Running** animation, which is a child asset of the **Zombie** model, and duplicate it such that a new copy appears in the **Project** window. Rename this copy `Run`.

13. Click on this animation and make sure to check the **Loop Pose** checkbox so that the animation runs in cycles.

14. Drag-and-drop the **Run** animation into the **Animator** tab. You should now have two animations in your FSM, with the default animation still as **Idle**; if you run the game, **Justin** should still just be idle. To make him switch animations, we need to do the following:

    1. Add some transitions to the **Run** animation from the **Idle** animation and vice versa.

    2. Trigger the transitions from a script.

15. You will want to switch from the **Idle** to the **Run** animation when the player's speed (as determined from the script) is greater than a small number (let's say 0.1 f). Since the variable for speed only lives in the script, we will need a way for the script to communicate with the animation, and we will do this with parameters.

16. In your **Animator** tab, note that the FSM we are developing lives in the **Base Layer** screen. While it is possible to add multiple animation layers by clicking on the + sign under **Base Layer**, this would allow the programmer to design multiple concurrent animation FSMs that could be used to develop varying degrees/levels of complex animation.

17. Add a new parameter by clicking on the + sign beside the **Parameters** panel. Select **float** from the list of datatypes. You should now see a new parameter. Name this `speed` as shown in the following screenshot:

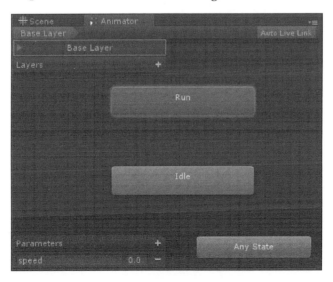

18. Right-click on the **Idle** Animation and select **Make Transition**. You will now see that a white arrow is visible, which extends from **Idle**, that tracks the position of your mouse pointer. If you now click on the **Run** animation, the transition from **Idle** to **Run** will lock into place.

19. Left-click on the little white triangle of the transition and observe the inspector for the transition itself. Scroll down in the **Inspector** window to the very bottom and set the condition for the transition to speed greater than 0.1, as shown in the following screenshot:

20. Make the transition from the **Run** animation cycle back to the **Idle** cycle by following the same procedure. Right-click on the **Run** animation to start the transition. Then, left-click on **Idle**. After this, left-click on the transition once it is locked into place. Then, when the transition is activated in **Conditions**, set its speed to less than 0.09.

Congratulations! Our character will now transition from **Idle** to **Run** when the speed crosses the 0.1 threshold. The transition is a nice blend from the first animation to the second over a brief period of time, and this is indicated in the transition graph.

Exploring in-place versus root motion animation

There are two ways of moving a character in a 3D world: using the in-place animation and the root animation. Each technique has some benefits and drawbacks depending on the effect you want to achieve. In a complicated character system, you may use both of these in different places.

- With the in-place animation, the character hierarchy is animated by the animation, whereas the root note of the character is not. To move your character about an axis, you need to move the root node in your script. Rotations to the root node of the character model will result in rotations to the character (and all the child objects of the character's hierarchy in the skeleton).

- With the root motion animation, both the character's hierarchy and the root node are animated by the animation. This means that you (as a programmer) need not translate nor rotate the root node about an axis because your animator will be responsible for doing that. Hence, this is a popular choice for some games but not all.

- Since our **Run** animation does not have root motion in it, we will move our character around in the script.

Adding the character script

Let's build the second half of our character system—the script that communicates the speed value to the FSM. We need to do this so that our characters can respond to the user's input.

1. Open the `PlayerControl.cs` script we wrote earlier for character motion.

2. We will use the `movespeed` variable as an approximation of the speed for the `speed` parameter. Around line 65, after this is calculated, we will pass the calculated speed to the `animator` component in the `speed` parameter. Don't forget to drag-and-drop the `animator` component on the character to the `animator` variable of the script as shown in the following code:

    ```
    if (_animator)
      _animator.SetFloat("speed",movespeed);
    ```

    Create a new, empty **GameObject** named `rotNode`. Assign it as a child to `Player1` and give it a local position of (0, -1, 0) and a local rotation of (0, 180, 0).

3. Attach the **Justin** model instance to the `player` class that we have already developed so far. Set its relative position to (0, -2, 0). Also, disable the mesh renderer component of `Player1` and its hat; we won't be needing these anymore since we will be using the **Justin** model.

4. Create a public animator reference inside `PlayerControls.cs`. Drag-and-drop the **Justin** instance to this variable so that it finds the animator component that has been attached there.

5. Make sure that the **Idle** animation has the **XZ** and **Y** rotation baked into the animation. This way, when the character is idle, its feet will not slide when the root motion is disabled.

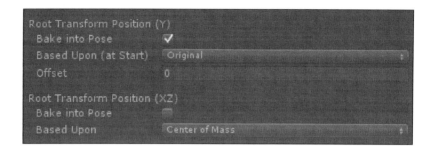

6. Switch to **Main Camera** and set the desired distance from 4 to 10.

Congratulations! Our main character model now walks about or stays idle according to the user input. Feel free to experiment with scaling the size of the **Justin** model and the speed of the player's motion in `PlayerControls.cs` to fine tune the speed and to reduce feet sliding.

Building a zombie racer animation FSM

Let's build an FSM that the racers in mission 2 will use. To start, let's develop the locomotion system.

1. Load the `TESTBED2` scene.

2. We will turn the racers into zombies for this level (this will motivate the player to run fast!). Drag-and-drop the **Zombie** model into the scene and scale it up to 3. Drag-and-drop the **Zombie** model on top of the `RacerA` GameObject. Do the same for another instance of **Zombie** but parent it to `RacerB`.

3. Create a new `AnimationController` object to drive the zombie's Mechanim FSM. Name the controller `ZombieControllerA`. Drag-and-drop the controller into the reference slot on the animator controller to associate it with Mechanim.

4. Click on `RacerA`, then click on the **Animator** tab to view the Mechanim preview panel.

5. Go back to `www.mixamo.com` to download and import the following two zombie movement animations. We will use different animations because each racer has a unique speed:

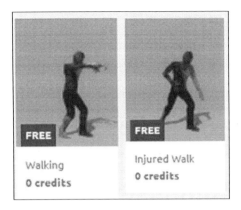

Walking
0 credits

Injured Walk
0 credits

6. Create a single animation FSM by dragging-and-dropping the zombie walk animation into the main window.

7. Create a second `AnimatorController` object named `ZombineController2`.

8. Drag-and-drop the `injured_walk` zombie animation into this window and save the scene.

9. Make sure these two animator controllers are correctly bound to the animator controllers of the two racers.

Congratulations! Now, when the race starts, the player will be chased by zombies! Think about how you might extend the racer NPC class such that if a zombie ever caught the player, it would switch to a grabbing animation to slow down the player's progress.

Building a quiz racer animation FSM

Let's build an FSM that the QuizNpc Prefabs in mission 2 will use. Again, let's develop the locomotion system to start.

1. Drag-and-drop an instance of the QuizNpc Prefab from the project library window into the scene.

2. Drag-and-drop an instance of the **Alexis** model (already downloaded) and place it beside QuizNpc. Disable the mesh renderer on QuizNpc so that it no longer renders, and parent the **Alexis** model to the QuizNpc GameObject.

3. Set **Alexis'** local position to (0, -1, 0).

4. Create a new AnimatorController named QuizNpcController. Drag-and-drop this controller from the **Project** pane directly into the AnimatorController field on the QuizNpc instance.

5. Select QuizNpc and then open the **Animator** panel to preview the empty FSM.

6. Drag-and-drop the **Idle** animation from the anims folder into the the panel.

7. The idle animation will play by default. When the player approaches QuizNpc, a pop up will be displayed. If an incorrect answer is chosen, this will have no bearing on the NPC's animation (although ideally, if we had access to more free animations, we would look for the one that conveyed disappointment).

   If a correct animation is chosen, QuizNpc will dance! To begin, drag-and-drop the **Gangnam** dance animation from the anims folder into the **Animator** window.

8. Create a transition from the **Idle** state to the **Gangnam** dance state by right-clicking on **Idle**, selecting **Make Transition**, and then left-clicking on **Gangnam** to complete the transition.

9. Click on the small + sign beside **Parameters** and create a new parameter named success of the type Boolean. We will use this to trigger the success animation from the script.

10. Left-click on the small white triangle of the transition and change the transition conditions to **Success** and **True**.

11. Drag-and-drop the **QuizNpc** GameObject back to the top of the QuizNpc Prefab in the **Project** tab. This will overwrite the pre-existing one with our new updates.

Make sure not to drag-and-drop the **QuizNpc** GameObject to the top of a different Prefab or else you will lose your other work!

12. We are going to need a new `PopupButton` action. Add another entry to the `popupAction` enumeration in `PopupButtonScript.cs`:

```
MakeNpcDance = 13
```

13. Add the following implementation of this action in the dispatch method of `PopupButtonScript`. If this action is dispatched, then find the NPC that has an ID that matches the ID of this correct pop-up card (passed through the side data of the pop-up response r), and set the `doSuccess` parameter on that NPC to `true`.

14. We do this by searching for all `QuizNpcHelpers` and then comparing the ID with the one requested from this pop up.

15. Then, when that NPC ticks through the `Update()` loop on its `QuizNpcHelper` script, the `true` param will be passed into the animator as shown in the following code:

```
case(popupAction.MakeNpcDance):
{
Object[] QuizNpcHelperObjects = Object.FindObjectsOfType(typeof(Qu
izNpcHelper));
foreach (Object item in QuizNpcHelperObjects)
{
   if ((item as QuizNpcHelper).GetQuizNpcId() == r.data. id)
   {
     (item as QuizNpcHelper).doSuccess = true;
   }
}
}
```

16. Inside `QuizNpcHelper`, declare the `Animator` component public. Then drag-and-drop the `Alexis` child object on top of this method to set up the reference association, as shown in the following line of code:

```
_animator = this.gameObject.GetComponent<Animator>();
```

17. Inside the `Update()` loop of the `QuizNpcHelper` script, pass the `doSuccess` parameter into the Mechanim FSM (if there is an animator component):

```
if (_animator)
{
  _animator.SetBool("success",doSuccess);
}
```

18. Now, go through the questions 1 to 5 of `popup_QuizNpcQuestion` from the `Chapter7` folder and add a new action of the `MakeNpcDance` type. Make sure to add the IDs 1 through 5 to the **ID** field of the `data` parameter for each of these new actions.

19. In `SetupMission2` present in the `Start()` method towards the end, add a line of code to pass the ID of the question, which this NPC will give the player, into the `QuizNpcHelper`. This way, when it's time to tell the NPC to change its animation, the pop-up card can find its NPC by searching for the one with the correct ID:

    ```
    QuizNpcInstance.GetComponent<QuizNpcHelper>().SetQuizNpcId(k);
    ```

20. Inside `InteractiveObject`, we add a simple `billboarding` behavior to the script so that `QuizNpc` can always face the player. If the billboard checkbox is enabled, we use the `Transform.lookat()` built-in method to make sure the NPC's transform always faces the player. We also fix up the local angles to makes sure the NPC doesn't look up or down if the NPC itself is really close to the player:

    ```
    if (billboard == true)
    {
        GameObject player = GameObject.Find("Player1");
        if (player != null)
        {
            this.transform.lookat(player.transform.position);
            this.transform.localEulerAngles = new Vector3(0.0f,
            this.transform.localEulerAngles.y, 0.0f);
        }
    }
    ```

Congratulations! `QuizNpc` now animates nicely and celebrates when the player responds correctly.

Exploring the Unity animation editor

While Mechanim is the preferred tool for character animations, it is not well suited to all of our animation needs. Unity provides a general-purpose animation tool that lets us script the position, orientation, and even the state of public variables on other scripts. This tool is well suited for simple animated objects and other in-game choreography. It uses a simpler non-visual animation system to play the animation but it still has many uses. Let's use this tool to add some animation to the starting banner.

1. Left-click on **pole2** of the `GiantFlagStart` Prefab instance.

2. Go to the **Window** menu and select **Animation**.

3. You will be presented with a timeline editor window, which will look similar to the following screenshot:

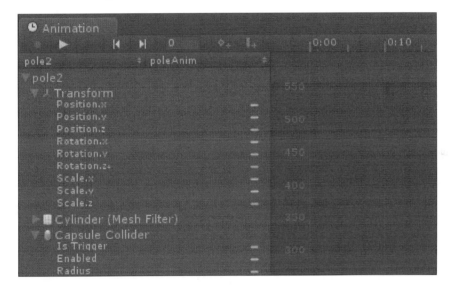

4. The animation editor window presents the user with a tool to author and preview custom animations inside of the Unity tool itself (rather than inside of a 3D modeling package). These animations can be applied to any GameObject that has public properties. All of the components, with the public variables on the GameObject that you have selected, will appear at the left-hand side of the screen. We can now apply the curve data to them over the timeline to build custom animations.

5. Click on the red record button in the upper-left corner of the animation editor to begin creating a custom animation.

6. The system will warn you that it needs to add the animation component (not animator) and that this will break your Prefab reference. Go ahead and allow the editor to add the component. We will update the Prefab once we are done.

7. The animation editor uses curves to modify data over time. Click on the x component of the transform and select **Add Curve**.

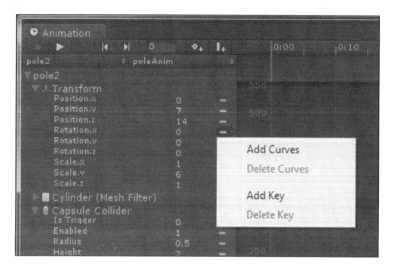

8. Now, by adding control points to these curves, we can animate the parameters of the object. Let's create a simple symmetric oscillation for the pole so that it shakes the banner in an interesting way.

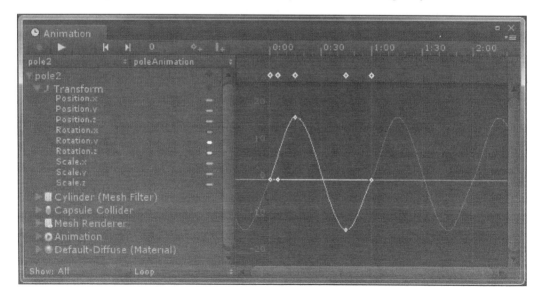

9. Once you are happy with your animation, toggle the record button to stop the recording. You will notice a new animation in your `assets` folder with the name you provided when you first clicked on record.

10. Drag-and-drop this animation into the first **Animation** field of the animation component on the pole object. Note that while this component supports playing and blending between multiple animations, it must be driven through scripting.

11. Make sure the **Play Automatically** checkbox is enabled to see your animation, without having to tie it to any script.

Congratulations! You have now successfully created a custom animation with the in-editor animation tool. To take this to the next level, feel free to explore the different playback modes on the animation assets themselves as well as ways of firing off methods from an animation curve with events. Remember, even slight changes to the properties of GameObjects in the scene will be recorded as animations

Summary

In this chapter, we learned a lot about animation in Unity. We integrated skinned models and animations from a third party. Using Mechanim, we created visually designed animation FSMs as well as the scripting-side integration. We upgraded our player, racer, and NPC game objects such that they now use these animated characters rather than the placeholder Prefabs.

We also learned a bit about the legacy animation system and the in-editor animation editor. We gained experience with this by creating a custom hand-tuned animation for a banner's flag pole and applied it to the game object so that it would play automatically. The game is looking much more polished now; a little visual appeal goes a long way!

In the next chapter, we will develop the final mission of the game, where we present the user with novel situations where they must use higher-order reasoning around the subject matter. This approach of thinking about the material from a bottom-up and top-down approach promotes consolidation of the material and is an effective way to drive learning in the user.

9
Synthesis of Knowledge

In this chapter, we will develop the third level in our e-learning game. This will be the final level in our game; the purpose of which is to help the user consolidate their learning by synthesizing new knowledge. The objective of this level is for the player, having now been promoted to ranger, to walk around the park tending to the needs of the visitors. The visitors will ask various questions or give hints about what they are thinking; the player needs to use higher-order reasoning to successfully interact with the game NPCs in suggesting an answer that has to do with state trivia. If the player answers correctly, we will reward the player in the game to promote learning.

We will reuse significant portions of technology from the first two missions to develop this chapter. In this chapter, we will cover the following topics:

- Understanding the mission three GameObjects
- Applying learning theory to mission three
- Creating the structure for mission three
- Modifying the pop-up system
- Creating the `NpcLocators` Prefab
- Creating the `CorrectResponse` Prefabs
- Modifying the quiz cards
- Adding another data condition
- Using the `setupLevel3` Prefab
- Creating the `AddScore` condition
- Creating the `ShowLevel3Results` response
- Creating the `Time` object
- Modifying the `LevelLogicObj` object
- Rewarding the player

Understanding the mission three GameObjects

In this level, we will implement a number of GameObjects and update others. Some of the game objects are listed as follows:

- `MissionMgr`: This GameObject will be present in this level, but we will not use a new mission to track the level progress. The `missionMgr` GameObject should still stick around in case we want to add secondary missions or side-quests to the game in the future.

- `Player`: The `Player` GameObject will need to have a working `playerData` component script attached to it. Since this level is completed upon achieving a certain score, and since scores (along with other statistics) are tracked in this data structure, we are required to implement `playerData`.

- `LevelLogicObj` : The `LevelLogicObj` GameObject is the main logic object that will track the players' score and the number of points that have been earned in this level, and will dispatch the pass condition pop up at the end of the level, assuming enough points have been acquired.

- `QuizCard` : The `QuizCard` GameObject creates a number of quiz cards (one for each state) that show the user a unique question or hint that the NPC will present to the player. The NPC will ask the player to choose a state that addresses their statement. If the correct answer is given, 500 points will be awarded to the player.

- `CorrectResponse`: The `CorrectResponse` GameObject creates a number of response cards that show your response (as the player) to the NPC when you give a correct response. These form the second half of the player to NPC interaction system in this level.

- `SetupLevel3`: The `SetupLevel3` GameObject is the Prefab that does the setup for `Mission 3` and starts the level.

- `Time` : The `Time` GameObject is a `clock` object. In this mission the pressure element will be provided by the race against the clock. If the clock reaches zero before 2,500 points are acquired, this class activates the failure condition pop-up dialog window.

Applying learning theory to mission three

The choice of a tourism-themed race against the clock was made to fill a number of e-learning game design requirements shown in the following diagram:

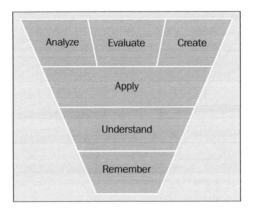

Effective learning requires manipulation of the subject matter at various levels of cognitive complexity. Hence, one powerful way to design mission content for our e-learning game is to deliver content that requires the player to interact with the subject matter in a variety of ways. Bloom's Taxonomy (aptly named after American educational psychologist Benjamin Bloom) gives us a pyramid heuristic that illustrates this concept. Relevant to this text; this taxonomy is a set of descriptive words that may be used to classify the different levels of cognitive complexity at which learning can occur.

Having used *remembering* as the underlying instructional mode in mission one (find the flags) and *applying* as the underlying instructional mode in mission two (quiz race), we increase the level of interaction with the subject matter in mission three to *analysis* and *evaluation* of the NPC's statements. We do this in order to encourage the player to synthesize an appropriate, subject-relevant reply. Through working with the same material on multiple levels, the player is naturally encouraged to remember, retain, and consolidate the learning that has taken place.

 For more information on Bloom's Taxonomy, feel free to review the information at `http://www.bloomstaxonomy.org/ Blooms%20Taxonomy%20questions.pdf` and `http://www. learningandteaching.info/learning/bloomtax.htm`.

Creating the structure for mission three

To begin, use LEVEL2 as a basis for developing LEVEL3 by performing the following instructions:

1. Copy and paste TESTBED2, and rename the copy TESTBED3.

2. Make sure that the _global GameObject from the original stays in the copy and that it is positioned at (0, 0, 0).

3. Rename the _level2 GameObject _level3.

4. Under _global, ensure that the player (named Player1), camera (named MainCamera), and Game (named Game) child objects can be found. Also, make sure that a GameObject of type GuiTexture named score is present.

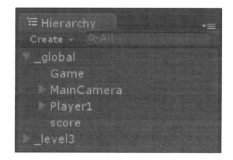

5. Under _level3, we will add the following level three-specific objects:

   ° Terrain

   ° setupLevel3

   ° Time

   ° NpcLocators

   ° LevelLogicObj

   ° Directional Light

Modifying the terrain

It is not necessary to modify the terrain from LEVEL2 to LEVEL3, but feel free to do so if you wish to add variety. The only constraint is that NpcLocators that you place need to be above the ground as before. This is because the NPCs precisely follow the path formed by the locators.

Adding visitors to the park

The primary interactions for this mission will come from the user talking with the NPCs. We will use a modified copy of the QuizNpc prefab from LEVEL2 to populate the final level. To implement this system, perform the following steps:

1. Copy the QuizNPC prefab from the Chapter7 folder into the Chapter 9 folder of the **Project** view.

2. Rename the new copy Npc.

Modifying the pop-up system

You will find three pop ups attached to the MainCamera object from the process of copying LEVEL2. These will need to be renamed and updated.

1. Rename popup_Level2Start to popup_Level3Start.

2. Update the text to read **You have been promoted to Park Ranger. Walk through the park and help the patrons by answering their questions. You must answer all questions correctly and earn 2500 points to win. Good luck!**

3. Ensure that this GameObject start behavior is enabled by default. The results of the steps performed so far are shown in the following screenshot:

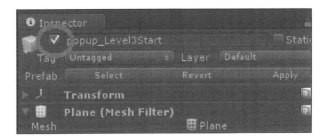

4. Rename popup_Level2Finish to popup_Level3Finish.

5. Update the text to read **Congratulations! Your state trivia knowledge is great! Your park is a success, and you WIN! Click okay to return to main menu.**

6. Ensure that the GameObject start behavior is disabled by default by unchecking it in the **Inspector** window.

7. Rename popup_Level3Repeat to popup_Level3Repeat in the **Inspector** window.

8. Update the text to read **Level 3. Your knowledge of state trivia is lacking. Try again! Click okay to reload**. We will connect the reload in *Chapter 10, An Extensible Game Framework Pattern in Unity*.

9. As usual, ensure this GameObject starts disabled by default by unchecking it in the **Inspector** window.

Congratulations! You have updated the pop ups that will appear at the start and completion of the level (for both success and failure conditions).

Creating the NpcLocators Prefab

The NpcLocators Prefab will hold a collection of locator GameObjects that the setupLevel3 prefab will use to pick locations for the NPCs. This should be a child of the _level3 object and can be constructed from the FlagLocators GameObject from LEVEL 2.

1. Locate the FlagLocators objects beneath the hierarchy of the _level3 object.

2. Rename the object to NpcLocators as shown in the following screenshot:

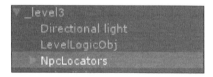

3. Feel free to mix up the locations of the objects to various places in the scene; this way, the player will not memorize the locations from LEVEL2. For variety, consider placing some on top of the mountains in the middle or around the periphery of the level.

Creating the CorrectResponse Prefabs

The CorrectResponse Prefabs are the pop ups that will be instantiated from the npcDialog (quiz cards) for LEVEL3. Create these according to the following steps:

1. Copy and paste the popup_QuizSuccessQuestion Prefab into a new folder in the folder named Chapter 9.

2. Create 50 unique CorrectResponse cards—one for each state/NPC dialog interaction.

3. We do not need to pass missionToken into missionMgr when this pop up destructs itself, so ensure that there is no missionToken attached (it will do no harm, but it is redundant).

4. Modify PopupButtonScript.cs and add an AwardPoints action. Make sure that when the button is clicked on each of these Prefabs, 500 points are awarded to the user. When the button is clicked, we simply find the player class and the playerData component, and then add these values to the score member variable as shown in the following code. Don't forget to add the action to the enumeration at the top of the file:

```
// inside Dispatch()
case(popupAction.AwardPoints):
{
  GameObject p = GameObject.Find ("Player1");
  if (p)
  {
    PlayerData pd = p.GetComponent<PlayerData>();
    if (pd)
    {
      pd.AddScore (r.data.id);
    }
  }
  break;
}
```

Modifying the quiz cards

The QuizCard pop-up window Prefab is the class that permits user interaction with an NPC; upon selecting the button corresponding to the correct response, the **CorrectResponse** window pop up will be instantiated.

1. Copy and paste a QuizCard Prefab from Chapter7 into a new folder in Chapter9. Name the new folder NpcQuestions.

2. Implement 50 unique NPC Dialog cards based on this Prefab, which in turn is based on the trivia content embedded in the `Flag` pop ups from `LEVEL1`; they will form the basis for the dialog in this mission.

3. Keep the associations to the `popup_QuizFailedQuestion` Prefab for the incorrect answers on these cards. For the correct selection, instantiate a unique and appropriate `CorrectResponse` Prefab.

4. Each `QuizCard` should have a unique `CorrectResponse` card. In this way, the player can see a contextually relevant response from you as you reply to the player. This gives an excellent opportunity to reinforce the learning material because it gives you a way to rephrase, restate, and reinforce the facts.

5. Make sure that each `CorrectResponse` card has an action to add points for every correct button click. Not only is this required for the mission to have an end condition, but this is also another way in which we reward the player for performing correctly. Remember, we can build a positive response in the learner with simple positive reinforcement with points and a dialog that furthers the story.

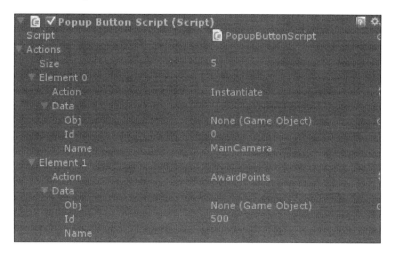

Congratulations! Associating each QuizNpc's **Instantiate** button action with the corresponding `CorrectResponse` card forms the brunt of the labor in creating mission three. Remember that Prefabs can only store associations with other Prefabs; be prudent to not drag-and-drop associations with actual instances of these classes themselves.

Adding another data condition

Just as we saw in *Chapter 7, Mission Two – Testing a Player's Learning*, when we created `listData npcCondition` which wrapped a list of GameObjects used to track racers in the race, we will need to create another type of wrapper in this mission; one for the initial score of the player. We can create this list with the following steps:

1. Copy and paste `listData.cs` into the folder named `Chapter9`. Rename the copy `floatData` as shown in the following screenshot:

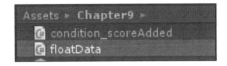

2. Update the declaration in the script to match the new name of the file.

3. Replace the `list<GameObject> _listData` variable with the following line of code:

```
public float _floatData;
```

Congratulations! You have now created a second `npcCondition` data wrapper. An instance of this will be required by the logic of this level to compute the points scored.

Using the setupLevel3 Prefab

The `setupLevel3` Prefab will be activated when the user presses the `popup_Level3Start` button. It will initialize the NPCs for the level, place them in random locations in the world, and set up the state tracking logic that determines if the player achieves success. Perform the following steps to use the `setupLevel3` Prefab:

1. Locate the Prefab named `setupLevel2` beneath `_level2`, and rename it `setupLevel3`. Duplicate the `SetupMissionTwo` script from mission two, and rename the duplicate to `SetupMissionThree`. Place the duplicate in the folder named `Chapter9` to keep your assets organized.

2. Add an instance of this script to the `setupLevel3` object.

3. Inside `MonoDevelop`, change the class declaration to `SetupMissionThree` so that it matches the name of the script as shown in the following code:

```
public class SetupMissionThree : MonoBehavior
```

4. We will use the same pattern to choose random NPC locators as we did for the QuizNpc locators in mission two. We will remove the `CorrectPopups` list, because each pop up will have a unique, correct pop up already associated with it in the editor.

5. At this point, open up `PopupPanel.cs`, and add the following line of code:

```
Public int id;
```

6. This ID will be used by the pop up to locate the NPC that dispatched it so that its animation can be updated on success.

7. In LEVEL3, we note the successful pass condition is when 2,500 points have been earned in addition to the points from levels one and two. In order to determine this, we need to remember the score at the beginning of the level so that we can calculate the delta.

8. At the top of `SetupMissionThree`, add an `initialScore` variable of type `npcCondition`. Since the level's complete processing will be handled by `npcDecisionMgr`, we need to store the score in a datatype that this system can operate on:

```
public npcCondition initialScore;
```

9. If a `Player` class can be found, extract the score from the `playerData` component, and store it in the `initialScore` component. Note that we need to cast the `npcComponent` base reference to `floatData` in order to access the `_floatData` member for storage.

10. The body of this method works in a manner similar to `SetupMissionTwo`, where it creates backups of the `QuizPrefab` and `SpawnPoint` lists. It diverges, however, when five random quiz cards are selected from the `QuizPrefab` list. We directly associate the `card` Prefab with the NPC to be instantiated as shown in the following code:

```
objectInteraction objInteraction = Npc.GetComponent<objectInteract
ion>();
   if (objInteraction)
     objInteraction.prefab = quizPrefab;
```

11. We also pass the ID value from the `QuizPrefab` card into the ID of `QuizNpcHelper`. We use this later when the `CorrectAnswer` pop up looks up the NPC that instantiated the card. At that time, we locate the NPC by ID and then pass `doSuccess` into its animator to make it dance as done in level two.

Congratulations! The `setupLevel3` Prefab is complete. We now have a class that will randomly pick a state quiz card and randomly spawn NPCs in the world to interact with the player.

Creating the AddScore condition

The `AddScore` condition will be used by `levelLogicObj` to track the points earned in this mission. Once the requisite number of points have been earned, this script will return `true`. This, in turn, will dispatch the response of showing the `Success` pop up via the `ShowLevel3Results` response script. Writing this script requires the following steps to be performed:

1. Create a new script named `condition_scoreAdded`. Change the base class from `MonoBehavior` to `npcCondition` as done with the other condition classes.

2. Add an instance of this script to `LevelLogicObj`.

3. Drag-and-drop this script instance into the second slot of `decisionMgr` on `LevelLogicObj` as shown in the following code:

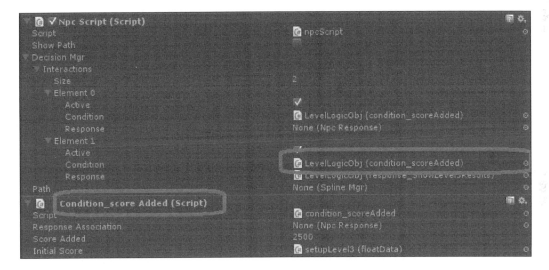

4. Inside the script, add an `int` datatype for `scoreAdded`; this is the number of points necessary for the condition to return `true`:

   ```
   public int scoreAdd;
   ```

5. Add an `npcCondition` called `initialScore`. Drag-and-drop the instance of this script from `setupLevel3` (remember the object that first stored the score on level start) into this reference as shown in the following code:

   ```
   public npcCondition initialScore {
   ```

6. If there is a `playerData` component on the player, then compute the score delta as the absolute value of the score minus the original score as shown in the following code:

```
if (p != null)
{
  float playerScore = Mathf.Abs (p.GetComponent<playerData>().
  score - (initialScore as floatData)._floatData);
  if ((int)playerScore >= scoreAdded )
    rval = true;
}
```

Congratulations! You have now created the condition for `npcDecisionMgr`, which will check for the number of points that have been earned in a given level.

Creating the ShowLevel3Results response

The `ShowLevel3Results` class will be used to show the success pop up (and some associated cleanup) if the user achieves enough points. It will be dispatched by `npcDecisionMgr` of `LevelLogicObj` in this level. Perform the following steps to create the `ShowLevel3Results` response:

1. Create a new `npcResponse` class named `response_ShowLevel3Results`. Change the parent class from `MonoBehavior` to `npcResponse`.

2. Open the scene file from the last gameplay level `TESTBED1`.

3. Copy the `popup_Level1Finished` Prefab by pressing *Ctrl + C*.

4. Open the scene file from the last gameplay level `TESTBED3`.

5. Paste this GameObject beneath the hierarchy of **MainCamera**. Rename the `popup_Level3Finish` object as shown in the following code:

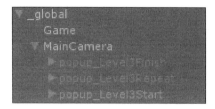

6. Add an instance of the `response_ShowLevel3Results` script to `LevelLogicObj`.

7. Drag-and-drop a reference to this script into the **Response** field beside `condition_addScore` in `decisionMgr` for `LevelLogicObj`.

8. Drag-and-drop a reference from `popup_Level3Finish` (inside the **MainCamera** hierarchy) into the `passPopup` field of the `response_ShowLevel3Results` script instance. In the `dispatch()` method of this script, enable the `passPopup` if it is valid, as shown in the following code:

```
if (passPopup != null)
passPopup.SetActive(true);
```

9. Then, on the **MainCamera**, invoke the `lookup()` method, to make sure the pop up is presented in a visually pleasing way, as follows:

```
GameObject camObj = Camera.main.gameObject
if ( camObj )
{
   camObj.GetComponent<GameCam>().LookUp();
}
```

10. Lastly, find the `clock` object named `Time`, and disable it with the following code. This is done to make sure the game doesn't show the out-of-time pop up while waiting for the success pop up:

```
GameObject clock = GameObject.Find("Time");
if (clock)
{
   clock.SetActive(false);
}
```

Creating the Time object

The `Time` object will implement the game's clock functionality in this level. If the time ever reaches zero, this class will display the mission failed pop up. Recall that the source of the added pressure this time around is the clock ticking down to zero. We want this because a little pressure makes the game fun and encourages cognitive flow. Perform the following steps to create the `Time` object:

1. Create a new script named `TimeScript.cs`. Add an instance of it to a new GameObject of type `GUIText`. Place `GUIText` on the left-hand side of the screen opposite the score. Note, this is done by adjusting the **PixelOffset** field of the `GUIText` component, and not by moving the transform (this is one of the few exceptions to the rule when placing objects in Unity).

2. A pixel inset of -60, -20 looks good at a screen resolution of 1024 x 768. Some of the settings for the GUIText component are shown in the following screenshot:

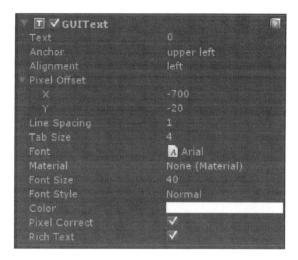

3. Add the following four variables to the script:
   ○ public GameObject failPopup: This variable will hold the reference to the pop up that is displayed if the user fails the mission by letting time run out.

   ○ public float starting_time: This variable will store the time when the timer should start before the level ends. Let's remember to set this to 120 seconds.

   ○ private float t: This variable will be used to store the current elapsed time.

   ○ public boolean timeElapsed = false: This Boolean variable will store whether or not this timer has reached zero at this time through the level.

   These variables can be declared in the following manner:

```
public GameObject failPopup;
public float starting_time;
private float t;
public boolean timeElapsed = false;
```

4. Inside the update() loop, we subtract the actual amount of time elapsed from t each time update() is called as shown in the following code:

```
t -= Time.deltaTime;
```

5. Once the time has elapsed, we tell the camera to look up and then show the fail pop up by setting its enabled flag to `true`. We set the local `timeElapsed` Boolean to `true` as well so that this response cannot show multiple times in a row accidentally:

```
if (t < 0.0f)
{
    GameObject camObj = Camera.main.gameObject;
    if (camObj) {
        camObj.GetComponent<GameCam>().LookUp();
        failPopup.SetActive(true);
        timeElapsed = true; }
}
```

6. Each time `update()` is called, the `Time` script will set the text of the `GUIText` component to be the string concatenation of `Time` and the elapsed time left (cast as an integer). We cast it to an integer to remove the trailing decimal points as shown in the following code:

```
this.gameObject.GetComponent<GUIText>().text = "Time : "+((int)
t).ToString ();
```

Congratulations! We now have a working game clock to add just enough game-play pressure to the player in the level. Consider adjusting the amount of time you give to the player based a difficulty setting in your game, the age of the player, or perhaps on how well the player is actually playing in the game. Remember, flow is achieved not only when the task at hand is somewhat challenging, but also in a scenario of moderate pressure.

Modifying the LevelLogicObj object

The LevelLogicObj object will track the condition when the player has achieved a high score that is enough to earn the **level finished** pop up and to win the game. To implement this with the technology we already have, we will perform the following steps:

1. In decisionMgr of npcScript on LevelLogicObj, set the number of interactions to 2. This is required because the LevelLogicObj object will process two interactions each frame.

2. Create an instance of a floatData condition on LevelLogicObj. Drag-and-drop this into the first condition. Make sure there is only one instance of this script on this object in the editor.

3. Create an instance of the condition_addScore condition on LevelLogicObj. Drag-and-drop this into the second condition. Set the scoreAdded variable on the condition to 2500, and drag-and-drop the setupLevel3 object into the initalValue reference to associate the initialValue condition component attached there into this component.

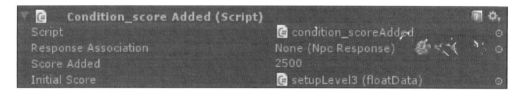

4. Create an instance of the response_ShowLevel3Results script on LevelLogicObj. Set the passPopup reference to the popup_Level3Finished pop up on the **MainCamera**.

5. Drag-and-drop this reference into the reference slot on the second interaction in npcDecisionMgr of the NPC script of LevelLogicObj.

   At this point, npcDecisionMgr on the LevelLogicObj object should look something like the following:

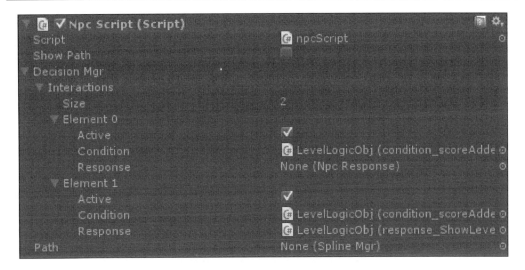

Congratulations! You have created the GameObject that implements the level logic of tracking the player's score and showing the finished Prefab if enough points are achieved on time.

Rewarding the player

We know that the more the positive responses and positive reinforcement we give to the player for performing well (showing that the material has been retained), the better will he or she retain and be able to recall it on demand. In this mission, we use a number of reinforcement techniques:

- The score is central to the player's success in this level. We give the player 500 points for each question that is answered correctly.

- The player is rewarded for further dialog from the player when he or she gives the correct answer. This further immerses the player with positive feedback and helps solidify a positive response.

- As with mission two, we make the NPC dance after the player gives a correct response. This is another example of a feel-good moment that helps condition a positive response in the player.

- Much of this feedback happens inside the `Action` parameter of the `CorrectResponse` pop up that is displayed for a particular trivia question, so make sure that you have the following actions in each of your `Response` Prefabs:

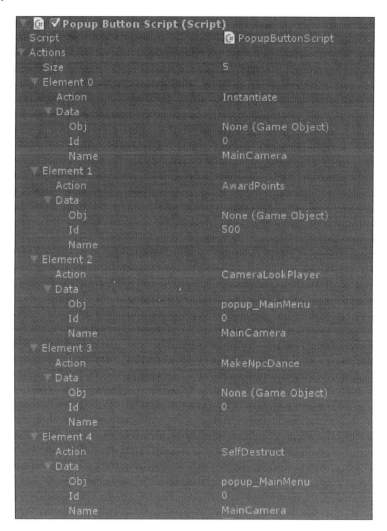

Summary

In this chapter, we applied learning theory and applied our existing technology from previous chapters in the development of the final level in our game. We developed the third mission of the three in our game, and by applying Bloom's Taxonomy to our learning outcomes, we developed content that encouraged the user to interact with the content at a high level, thus encouraging learning. This completes the final stage in our e-learning game. In the final chapter, we will tie these three levels together with the rest of the game framework while refactoring some systems during the process.

10
An Extensible Game Framework Pattern in Unity

In the final chapter of the book, we will take all of the pieces we have developed so far and assemble them into our final game! To do this, we will need to complete a framework for loading and unloading individual scene files, connect that system into level transition logic, and restructure a number of classes and Prefabs in our scene files so that they work together using this pattern. We will also develop the code necessary to ensure that the references that were created inside the editor can be reconnected as necessary when scenes are streamed in. Having a consistent pattern with which we can organize our scripts based on when they are needed gives us a reusable and extendible pattern we can use to quickly add new levels to our game. Not only this, but it can be used as a framework for future games that you develop!

In this chapter, we will cover the following topics:

- Load additively
- Using delete/load patterns
- Refactoring our work

Load additively

Recall from *Chapter 4, Mission One – Future Proofing the Code*, that Unity3D supports the development of games that span multiple scene files. One benefit of splitting a game up into multiple scene files is that we (as programmers) can assign different lifespans to objects based on the scene file they belong to.

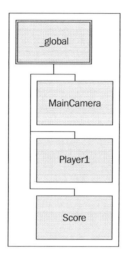

The MAIN scene file is designed to not only be the entry point of our game, but it also contains the _global GameObject. This GameObject acts as the parent of a hierarchy of objects that have persistent scope throughout the game. The following GameObjects should have global scope:

- MainCamera: This is the camera to which the scene will be rendered

- Player1: This is the name of the GameObject that is the playable character or the hero of the game

- Score: This is a GUIText element that displays the number of points the player has acquired so far

Every other GameObject will exist in one of the three scene files for the game— LEVEL1, LEVEL2, or LEVEL3. Using the Application.LoadLevelAdditive() method, we can make sure each playable level has both the objects from the persistent _global scene file and the level-specific objects from the scene. This is because Application.LoadLevelAdditive() combines the GameObjects from the loaded scene with the GameObjects that are already loaded. Contrast this with Application.LoadLevel(), which will destroy the previously instantiated scene file and all of its GameObjects before loading the new scene, and the reason for loading additively is clear; we want both sets of GameObjects to be loaded so we use the additive load!

Of course, we need to be absolutely sure that there are no duplicate objects in the _global scene file and the level-specific scene, or else logical errors will ensue. Let's ensure we can do this now by updating the GameMgr script as follows:

1. In GameMgr.cs, ensure that the eGameState enumeration has entries for Invalid, MainMenu, Level1, Level2, and Level3. We will delegate responsibility for switching levels to this class instance. Each of these enumerated values will correspond to the scene file with the same name. Through this enumeration, we will inform the GameMgr script which scene file to load:

```
public enum eGameState
{
  eGS_Invalid = -1, //enum for error case
  eGS_MainMenu = 0,
  eGS_Level1 = 1,
  eGS_Level2 = 2,
  eGS_Level3 = 3
};
```

2. In the Update() loop, we ensure that there is no longer any auto state-changing code. This method should be empty at this point. For the most prompt level, change the signal rather than letting this system update the level when it detects a change. We will call ChangeLevel() directly from the level complete pop ups when a change is required.

Using delete/load patterns

Having planned how to organize our GameObjects into globally persistent and level-specific lifespans, we must further update GameMgr.cs to ensure that only the current level is loaded at any time. To do this, perform the following steps:

1. In GameMgr.cs, inside the ChangeState() method, the first thing we do is tell the game to delete any potential level-specific GameObject hierarchies that may be loaded:

```
if (GameObject.Find("_level1")
  Destroy (GameObject.Find ("_level1"));
if (GameObject.Find("_level2")
  Destroy (GameObject.Find ("_level2"));
if (GameObject.Find("_level3")
  Destroy (GameObject.Find ("_level3"));
```

2. Inside the `switch` statement that `ChangeState()` implements, we signal a `LoadLevelAdditive()` call when changing to LEVEL1, LEVEL2, or LEVEL3. However, when switching to MAIN, we simply need to destroy the `_level1`, `_level2`, and `_level3` GameObjects since `_global` remains persistent throughout.

3. Recall that each level-specific scene file must be constructed according to the pattern `_leveln` (where n is 1 for LEVEL1, 2 for LEVEL2, and 3 for LEVEL3). This is because while Unity does provide a function for loading a scene file additively, it does *not* provide a way to unload a scene file once the objects have been loaded. To accomplish this, we perform the following steps:

    1. Ensure that we construct our levels with a single parent GameObject at the root.

    2. Name the root GameObject so that it follows a consistent pattern. We use `_level1`, `_level2`, and `_level3` for our scene files.

4. This permits us to implement an unload scene file functionality by simply destroying the root object. Doing this will destroy the object and all the objects that are children of its hierarchy.

Congratulations! You have now finished updating the `GameMgr` system to handle loading and unloading scene files. This system of loading additively and naming the scene files consistently may be extended to other gameplay levels.

Refactoring our work

Now that we have a fully functional system for loading and unloading scene files, we will dedicate our attention to the integration and refactoring of the remaining GameObjects, hierarchies, and scripts.

The pop-up system

To refactor our pop-up system, perform the following steps to complete the moving of our game content from the `testbed` scene file to the MAIN scene file.

Updating level 3 pop ups

Let's begin by refactoring the pop-up panel system:

1. Under **_global**, ensure that the player (named **Player1**), camera (named **MainCamera**), and game (named **Game**) child objects can be found. Also make sure that a GameObject of type GUITexture named **score** is present as shown in the following screenshot:

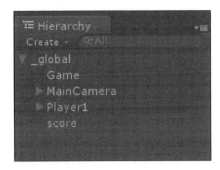

2. We will change the behavior of the pop ups that are shown at the start and completion of each level. Rather than instantiating them from a Prefab, we will add them at design time in the editor and selectively activate and deactivate them as necessary. This will make the task of refactoring the pop-up system more straightforward.

3. Load the TESTBED3 scene file. Find the MainCamera GameObject, and open the **Hierarchy** tab to display the UI pop up's child objects.

4. Press the *Shift* key, select all of the pop ups, and copy them with *Ctrl + C*.

5. Load the MAIN scene file. Select the MainCamera GameObject, and paste the level 3 pop ups with *Ctrl + V*. This will paste the pop ups that we copied from step 4.

6. Now, we need to change the behavior of the buttons. Starting with the pop up named **popup_Level3Start**, select this panel, and open the **Button1** hierarchy.

7. Change the actions of this button to `CameraLookPlayer()` so that the camera looks down on the start of the level, and call `DisableObject(popup_Level3Start)` so that this panel disappears but remains attached to the `MainCamera` GameObject persistent in `_global`.

8. Next, select the **popup_Level3Finish** panel, and open the **Button1** hierarchy.

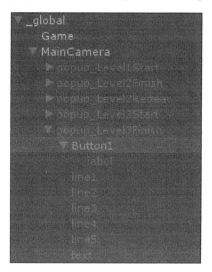

9. Change the first action of this button to `LoadLevelMainMenu` (to tell `GameMgr` to unload `Level3`, leaving just `_global`).

10. Change the next action to `HideGameObject(popup_Level3Finish)` to disable update and rendering of this panel, while still leaving it attached to the `MainCamera` GameObject persistent in `_global`.

11. Change the last action to `EnableObject(popup_MainMenu)` to make the main menu show up again.

12. Lastly, click on the **popup_Level3Repeat** panel, and open the **Button1** hierarchy.

13. Change the first action to `CameraLookUp()` to point the camera towards the sky (which makes the pop ups show up in a visually appealing way).

14. Change the next action to `LoadLevel3`. This will tell the `GameMgr` script to destroy the `_level3` GameObject (and all of its children), and then reload the `_level3` GameObject, thereby resetting its state.

15. Change the final action to `DisableObject(popup_Level3Repeat)` to hide this panel while still leaving it attached to the `MainCamera` GameObject persistent in `_global`.

Congratulations! You have finished updating the pop ups for `Level3`. Let's move on to pop ups of `Level2`.

Updating level 2 pop ups

Now that pop ups of level 3 are updated, let's follow the same procedure to update the pop ups for the second level.

1. Load the TESTBED2 scene file. Find the MainCamera GameObject, and open hierarchy to display the UI pop up's child objects.

2. Press *Shift*, select all of the pop ups, and copy them with *Ctrl + C*.

3. Load the MAIN scene file. Select the MainCamera GameObject, and paste the level 3 pop ups with *Ctrl + V*.

4. Now we need to change the behavior of the buttons. Starting with **popup_Level2Start**, select this panel, and open the **Button1** hierarchy.

5. Change the first action of this button to EnableObject(raceStarterPref ab). Set the reference to raceStarterPrefab by dragging-and-dropping it from the **Project** tab directly into the data field of the button's action. This way, the button will instance a GameObject from this Prefab on click.

6. Change the second action of this button to EnableObject(setupLevel2Pre fab). In a similar fashion as earlier, set the reference to setupLevel2Prefab by dragging-and-dropping it from the **Project** tab directly in to the data field of the button's action. This way, the button will instance a GameObject from the Prefab on click.

7. Change the third action to CameraLookPlayer() so that the view will track the hero as the character moves in the world.

8. Change the last action of this button to HideGameObject(popup_ Level2Start) to hide this panel while still leaving it attached to the MainCamera GameObject persistent in _global.

9. Next, select the **popup_Level2Finished** button, and open up the **Button1** hierarchy.

10. Change the first action of this button to CameraLookUp(). This will orient the camera to a point above the player so that the subsequent pop ups will display in a visually appealing way.

11. Change the next action of this button to `LoadLevel3` (to tell `GameMgr` to unload `Level2` by destroying the root GameObject instance, and then load `Level3`). Throughout this process, `_global` and all of its child objects will be preserved.

12. Change the last action of this button to `HideGameObject(popup_Level2Finish)`. This will disable the rendering of this panel while still leaving it attached to the `MainCamera` GameObject persistent in `_global`.

13. Lastly, select the **popup_Level2Repeat** panel, and open the **Button1** hierarchy.

14. Change the first action to `CameraLookUp()` to point the camera towards the sky (which makes the pop ups show up in a visually appealing way).

15. Change the next action to `LoadLevel2`. This will tell the `GameMgr` script to destroy the `_level2` GameObject (and all of its children), and then reload the `_level2` GameObject, thereby resetting its state.

Congratulations! You have finished updating the pop ups for level 2. Let's move on to the pop ups of level 1.

Updating level 1 pop ups

Now that pop ups of level 2 are finished, let's update and modify the pop ups for level 1.

1. We need to create a start pop up for level 1 that matches the pattern of the other two levels.

2. Copy `popup_Level2Start` from `MainCamera`, and paste it on `MainCamera` as well.

3. Rename the copy as `popup_Level1Start`.

4. At this point in time, your `MainCamera` hierarchy should look similar to the following screenshot:

5. Set the first action on `Button1` to `CameraLookPlayer()` so that when the level starts, the camera will track the hero.

6. Set the second action on `Button1` to `DisableObject(popup_Level1Start)`. This will hide this panel while still leaving it attached to the `MainCamera` GameObject persistent in `_global`.

7. We will not need to allow the user to repeat level 1. Since there is no fail condition, we will not need a repeat pop up for level 1. The level complete pop up will be dynamically allocated as a reward for finishing the level 1 mission of returning flags to the monument as originally designed.

8. To support easy programmatic access to these pop ups, we will write a `PopupMgr` script to store references to these pop-up objects. This class will then be used to access these pop ups for easy enabling and disabling.

9. Create a new script with the C# script wizard named `PopupMgr`, and attach it to the `MainCamera` instance in the `_global` hierarchy.

10. Give this script eight public references to the following GameObject pop ups:

    ° `public GameObject MainMenu;`

    ° `public GameObject Level1Start;`

    ° `public GameObject Level2Start;`

    ° `public GameObject Level2Finish;`

    ° `public GameObject Level2Repeat;`

    ° `public GameObject Level3Start;`

    ° `public GameObject Level3Finish;`

    ° `public GameObject Level3Repeat;`

    These are references to the actual pop-up objects that the `PopupMgr` script will enable and disable as the game moves from level to level.

11. Make sure to assign the actual instances of these GameObjects to these variables in the `PopupMgr` script by either dragging-and-dropping them in or selecting them from the selection panel.

Congratulations! The pop-up system has been fully refactored for our game. As level 1 is now fully functional, let's turn our attention to integrating the rest of TESTBED2 and TESTBED3 into our game.

Refactoring level 2

At this point, our project is composed of two scene files; a main scene file that contains the persistent _global GameObject hierarchy, and the LEVEL1 scene file that contains the _level1 hierarchy for all of the level 1 scripts and objects. While TESTBED2 and TESTBED3 were designed to be played as standalone levels, our final game framework is not. Hence, we now need to port and integrate the remaining game content into this pattern.

1. Open the TESTBED2 scene file into the editor. Locate the **_global** and **_level2** GameObjects in the **Hierarchy** tab.

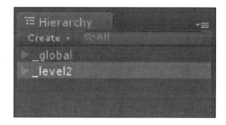

2. Copy the _level2 GameObject with *Ctrl + C*.

3. Create a new scene file named LEVEL2.

4. Paste the _level2 object hierarchy into this scene with *Ctrl + V*.

5. You now have an appropriate scene file package for level 2. Let's repeat the process for level 3.

6. Open the TESTBED3 scene file into the editor. Locate the **_global** and **_level3** GameObject in the **Hierarchy** tab.

7. Copy the _level3 GameObject with *Ctrl + C*.

8. Create a new scene file named LEVEL3.

9. Paste the _level3 object hierarchy into this scene with *Ctrl + V*.

You now have an appropriate scene file package for level 3.

Implementing a system to connect object references

Level 1 signals level 2 to load when the **Level 1 completes** pop up's **Next** button is pressed; it signals for the _level1 GameObject to be destroyed and the _level2 GameObject to be loaded from the LEVEL2 scene file. We must refactor the start-up logic of _level2 so that we can find and connect some object references to GameObjects in the _global hierarchy.

1. Create a new script named Level2Extras, and attach an instance of it to the _level2 GameObject. This script will be used to directly access certain GameObjects inside _level2 for enabling and disabling.

2. Give the Level2Extras script the following three public GameObject references; these are the assorted GameObjects that this script will be in charge of activating:

    ```
    public GameObject raceStartup;
    public GameObject setupLevel2;
    public GameObject LevelLogicObj;
    ```

3. Drag-and-drop the LevelLogicObj object from the _level2 GameObject hierarchy into the LevelLogicObj reference of the Level2Extras script.

4. Drag-and-drop the setupLevel2 GameObject from the _level2 GameObject hierarchy into the setupLevel2 reference of the Level2Extras script.

5. Drag-and-drop the raceStartup GameObject from the _level2 GameObject hierarchy into the raceStartup reference of the Level2Extras script.

6. At this point your Level2Extras script should look something like the following:

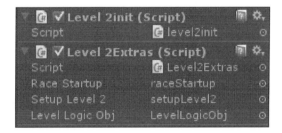

7. Observe that as you click on the populated references inside `Level2Extras`, Unity highlights the GameObject instances with a unique yellow border so that you can quickly find the actual object instances that are connected in the hierarchy.

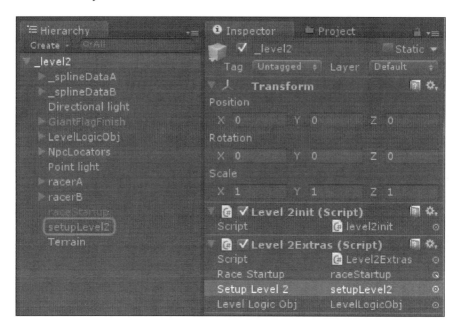

8. Now that `Level2Extras` has been properly configured, create another script named `Level2Init`, and add an instance of it to the `_level2` GameObject.

9. The `level2Init` script will use the `Level2Extras` script as an interface to find specific GameObjects and connect them into the appropriate level 2 pop ups. This needs to happen since the pop ups are global; they cannot preserve references to objects that are dynamically loaded from later levels.

10. In the `start()` method of `Level2Init`, the script attempts to locate the `Player` GameObject, named as either `Player` or `Player1`:

```
GameObject playerObj = GameObject.Find ("Player1");
if (playerObj == null)
  playerObj = GameObject.Find ("Player");
```

11. If a suitable player object is found, the code sets the initial position and the orientation for the player. This is so that when level 2 starts, the player begins at the starting line of the race:

```
if (playerObj != null)
{
  playerObj.transform.position =
    new Vector3(-110.0f, 3.0f, 166.0f);
  p.GetComponent<playerControls>().moveDirection =
    new Vector3(1.0f, 0.0f, 0.0f);
}
```

12. In the `Update()` method of `Level2Init`, the class attempts to find the `MainCamera` GameObject. If it can be found, the `PopupMgr` script component is stored:

```
GameObject camObj = GameObject.Find ("MainCamera");
if (camObj)
{
  PopupMgr ppm = camObj.GetComponent<PopupMgr>();
```

13. If an instance of the `PopupMgr` script can be found on this GameObject, we activate `popup_Level2Start` and deactivate `popup_Level2Finish` and `popup_Level2Repeat`. By setting these objects to active, we tell Unity that these scripts should be allowed to call their internal `Update()` methods. Conversely, when setting `SetActive(false)`, we can tell Unity to suspend scripts as needed:

```
// set up the level2 popups initial state
ppm.Level2Finish.SetActive(false);
ppm.Level2Repeat.SetActive (false);
ppm.Level2Start.SetActive(true);
```

14. Then we store a reference to the `PopupMgrScript` on the `popup_Level2Start` GameObject for later use:

```
PopupButtonScript pbs =
  ppm.Level2Start.transform.FindChild
  ("Button1").gameObject.GetComponent<PopupButtonScript>();
```

15. We also store a reference to the `Level2Extras` script for easy access later in the method:

```
Level2Extras l2x = GetComponent<Level2Extras>();
```

16. If the `Level2Extras` component can be found, we need to associate `setupLevel2` to the `popup_Level2Start` instance on its first button action. Then, we associate `raceStartup` to the `popup_Level2Start` instance on its second button action:

```
pbs.actions[0].data.obj = l2x.setupLevel2;
pbs.actions[1].data.obj = l2x.raceStartup;
```

17. Next, we try to cache a reference to the `response_ShowRaceResultsPopup` component that is attached to `LevelLogicObj` inside `Level2Extras`:

```
response_ShowRaceResultsPopup rrp = l2x.LevelLogicObj.
GetComponent<response_ShowRaceResultsPopup>();
```

18. If the race results pop-up component can be found, we connect the `player`, `GameMgr`, `PassPopup`, and `FailPopup` to this script. This will allow this response script to operate correctly during the race:

```
rrp.player = GameObject.Find ("Player1");
rrp.gm = GameObject.Find ("Game").GetComponent<gameMgr>();
rrp.passPopup = ppm.Level2Finish;
rrp.retryPopup = ppm.Level2Repeat;
```

19. After this, the `Level2Init` script will destroy itself. This stops the init logic from running more than once when `_level2` is loaded. If `_level2` is ever reloaded (during a restart perhaps), this script will be re-instanced when `_level2` is loaded again.

Congratulations! The logic for configuring the missing references of level 2 on startup has been completed. Let's move our attention to how the mission 2 logic is actually set up.

Updating the SetupMission2 script

Prior to integrating the missions together, we developed our game so that mission 1, mission 2, and mission 3 individually selected five states from a bank of 50. While this is fine for playing them in isolation, we need to add continuity of the state selections across all three levels. We will do this by storing the selections when they are made in level 1, and then by restoring them as level 2 and level 3 are loaded.

1. To begin, load the LEVEL1 scene file. Find the Monument GameObject, and open the SetupMissionOne script.

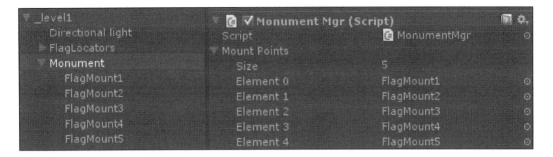

2. In the `SetupMission()` method, on line 65, we find the `player` GameObject named either `Player` or `Player1`:

```
GameObject playerObj = GameObject.Find ("Player1");
if (playerObj == null)
   p = GameObject.Find ("Player");
```

3. If a player can be found, we cache a reference to the `PlayerData` component attached to it:

```
pd = p.GetComponent<playerData>();
```

4. If there are any flag choices in `PlayerData` at this point, we clear them. This is a reasonable assumption to make in level 1 as it is the first gameplay level that we encounter. The subsequent levels will access these values when populating their scenes. Clearing the `flagChoices` array before use is a good defensive practice so that we don't accidentally end up with more flag instances in the level than intended:

```
if (pd.flagChoices.Count > 0)
   pd.flagChoices.Clear();
```

5. In the `SetupMission()` method, on line 92, as the initial set of flags are chosen, we store the flag index in the `playerData` component. Here, they will be carried with the player through level 2 and level 3:

```
if (pd != null)
   pd.flagChoices.Add (index);
```

6. Now that the first mission has been successfully updated to store flag choices in `PlayerData`, we shall now move our attention towards refactoring level 2 and level 3 to use this data.

7. In the `Start()` method of the `SetupMissionTwo` script, while we are iterating over the flags, we check if there is a `PlayerData` component on the player. If one can be found, we assign the flag index from the list in `PlayerData` to the variable index rather than a randomly assigned one:

    ```
    if (pd != null)
      index = pd.flagChoices[k];
    ```

Congratulations! This completes the required updates for level 2. Now, when starting the game and selecting **NEW**, level 1 will be shown initially, and upon completion, the game will dynamically load level 2. Let's continue updating the code in the same light as we integrate and refactor level 3.

Refactoring level 3

When level 2 signals level 3 to load (when the player pressed the level 3 pop up's **Continue** button), it signals for the `_level2` Gameobject to be destroyed and the `_level3` GameObject to be loaded from the LEVEL3 scene file. We must refactor the start up logic of `_level3` so that we can find and connect some object references to GameObjects in the `_global` hierarchy. To accomplish this, perform the following steps:

1. Create a new script named `Level3Extras`, and attach an instance of it to the `_level3` GameObject. This script will be used to directly access certain GameObjects inside `_level3` for enabling and disabling.

2. Give the `Level3Extras` script the following single public GameObject reference. The `Level3Extras` script needs a reference to the `setupLevel3` object so that it can connect this reference to the appropriate pop-up button later on in the script:

    ```
    public GameObject setupLevel3;
    ```

3. Drag-and-drop the `SetupLevel3` GameObject from the `_level3` GameObject hierarchy into the `SetupLevel3` reference of the `Level3Extras` script.

4. Now that `Level3Extras` has been properly configured, create another script named `Level3Init`, and add an instance of it to the `_level3` GameObject.

5. The `level3Init` script will use the `Level3Extras` as an interface to find specific GameObjects and connect them into the appropriate level 3 pop ups. This needs to happen since the pop ups are global; they cannot preserve references to objects that are dynamically loaded from subsequent levels in the game.

6. In `Level3Init`, we first try to find a reference to a GameObject named `MainCamera`:

```
GameObject go = GameObject.Find ("MainCamera");
```

7. If the `MainCamera` GameObject can be found, we try to cache a reference to the `PopupMgr` script component attached to it:

```
if (go)
{
   PopupMgr ppm = go.GetComponent<PopupMgr>();
```

8. If the `PopupMgr` script can be found, we set the initial state of the UI pop ups for level 3. As before, we use `SetActive(false)` to suspend the `Update()` loop of some scripts and `SetActive(true)` to enable others. Namely, we deactivate `popup_Level3Finish` and `popup_Level3Restart`. We then activate `popup_Level3Start` so that the level starts with the relevant UI displayed. Note that at this point, the camera is looking up from `popup_Level2Finish`:

```
if (ppm)
{
   ppm.Level3Finish.SetActive (false);
   ppm.Level3Repeat.SetActive(false);
   ppm.Level3Start.SetActive(true);
```

9. Next, we try to cache a reference to `PopupButtonScript`, which is attached to `button1` child of `popup_Level3Start`. We use `transform.FindChild()` to search for an object in a hierarchy by name. Once we find it, we can get the component for `PopupButtonScript` itself using `GetComponent()`:

```
PopupButtonScript pbs =
   ppm.Level3Start.transform.FindChild
   ("Button1").gameObject.GetComponent<PopupButtonScript>();
```

10. Now that we have `PopupButtonScript`, we assign a reference to the `Level3Extras` script (attached to this object) to the data field of the first action of `PopupButtonScript`. This way, when the button is clicked, the `EnableObject` action will operate on the `SetupLevel3` GameObject (accessed from `Level3Extras`):

```
Level3Extras l3x = GetComponent<Level3Extras>();
if (l3x)
{
  pbs.actions[0].data.obj = l3x.setupLevel3;
}
```

11. Next, we connect the `popup_Level3Finish` pop up to the `response_ShowLevel3Results` component. This will allow `LevelLogicObj` to display the level complete UI:

```
GameObject llo = GameObject.Find ("LevelLogicObj");
if (llo != null)
{
    llo.GetComponent<response_ShowLevel3Results>().passPopup =
    ppm.Level3Finish;
}
```

12. In `_level3`, the fail condition is triggered from the `Timer` GameObject, when the time remaining reaches zero. To enable this component to display the `popup_Level3Repeat` UI, we must connect them together via the `PopupMgr` script:

```
GameObject TimeObj = GameObject.Find ("Time");
if (TimeObj != null)
{
  TimeObj.GetComponent<TimeScript>().failPopup =
    ppm.Level3Repeat;
}
```

13. Congratulations! The initial setup for `_level3` is now complete. Let's turn our attention to updating the `SetupMissionThree()` script. To begin, locate this script instance attached to the `setupLevel3` object. As with the previous two examples, this script is responsible for connecting the missing references between pop ups that have global persistence and the GameObjects that they refer to inside of specific level scene files—inside `_level3` in this instance.

14. At the beginning of `Start()`, we search for the `Player` GameObject (named either `Player` or `Player1`). If it is found, we store a reference to the `PlayerData` component for later use:

```
playerData pd = null;
GameObject go = GameObject.Find ("Player1");
if (go == null)
  go = GameObject.Find ("Player");
if (go != null)
{
  pd = go.GetComponent<playerData>();
}
```

15. Still in the `start` method, in the block where five random cards are chosen, we check for the presence of the `PlayerData` component on the player. If there is no data, it means we are playing this mission in standalone mode, and so we should use five randomly chosen indices. If, however, `PlayerData` has information contained therein, it means that we should use those indices to populate our world to ensure the flag choices are consistent with the previous level:

```
if (pd != null)
  index = pd.flagChoices[k];
```

Congratulations! Mission 3 has been updated now to use the flag choices that were randomly chosen in LEVEL1 and reused in LEVEL2. With that, your e-learning game is complete! Please take a moment to pause, look at how far we have come since *Chapter 1, Introduction to E-Learning and the Three Cs of 3D Games*, and give yourself a pat on the back for a job well done!

Playing and distributing your game

Now that your game is done, we need to package it so that others can play it outside of the Unity development environment. Unity is a cross platform engine, and while that does mean that you can design once and build a game that runs on many types of hardware, let's build a version that works for Windows (the preferred development hardware for this text).

1. Open up the MAIN scene from the completed project.
2. Select **Build Settings** from the **File** drop-down menu.

3. On the **Build Settings** screen, make sure that the four scene files for our game have been added to the build. Namely, ensure that **MAIN**, **LEVEL1**, **LEVEL2**, and **LEVEL3** are present.

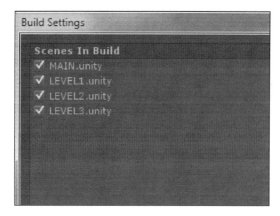

4. To add a scene file to the build, open each scene file in the main Unity application, and then under this **Build Settings** screen, click on **AddCurrent**.

5. Simply select the platform you wish to build for from the options on the bottom-left corner of the **Build Settings** panel, and then click the **Build** button. A dialog box will pop up asking you where to save your .exe file and with what name. Our game is called Geography Quest.

6. Once the build is complete, navigate to that folder, and you have a game you can run with a double-click of the mouse! Don't forget to distribute the GeographyQuest_Data folder along with the GeographyQuest.exe program.

Reflecting on e-learning and game design

Let's review what we have implemented so far with this game in terms of e-learning strategy and technique. Our game has four scene files (MAIN, LEVEL1, LEVEL2, and LEVEL3). In the MAIN scene file lives the _global object hierarchy that holds the singleton class instances in the game: systems such as the Player, Camera, Game, and Light. Not only is this scene file the entry point to our game, but these objects persist as other level-specific scenes are loaded and unloaded.

Level 1 is the Find the Flags mission, wherein the user is taught about state names, state flags, and state trivia. As each flag is picked up, a trivia card is presented and placed in the inventory. The user can then click on these cards and review the trivia card throughout the game.

Level 2 is the Zombie Race level, wherein the user is quizzed on their retention of the material from Level 1. Adding an element of pressure to the game is the fact that zombies are chasing the player (they want to win the race before you do). Along the race, the player must interact with NPCs who quiz them on state flags. We explore the concept of cognitive flow and how to encourage the player to achieve this state of total engagement. We determine that to maximize flow, we need to design testing scenarios with tasks that are moderately challenging and that contain an element of tension or pressure.

Level 3 is the Park Ranger level, where the player has to race against a clock, find park visitors, and apply their knowledge to help each one with their question. Manipulating learned material at a level higher than memorization is an activity known to support long-term learning.

While this three-stage loop is used in the traditional classroom as well as in e-learning games to teach facts, it is also a great structure to teach game mechanics or other types of skills to the learner.

Summary

We have taken the components from `mission1`, `testbed2`, and `testbed3`, and integrated them together into one seamless game. The final game is composed of four scene files, each of which contains a single GameObject hierarchy. The top object in the hierarchy is given a name consistent with the scene filename. Some refactoring of existing systems was then required to fix up the classes at initialization time so that no missing or dangling references would be incurred.

Congratulations! We have now finished our e-learning game framework. Not only did we develop a game that exercises good teaching and learning pedagogy, we also implemented a number of core gameplay systems for the interactive elements in the game. While we proved the technology with a geography trivia game, the framework could be adapted and re-skinned for other topics. Logical potential directions for future work could include adding levels beyond the initial three. This could be done by developing more interactive objects for your game by fleshing out your library of condition-and-response classes for the decision manager, optimizing your code so that it can run efficiently on resource constrained platforms such as smartphones, or adding more polish to the game such as through audio or particles. No matter what, make sure you have fun in the process!

Index

Symbols

3D game
  camera code 15
  camera system 11
  character system 11
  controls system 11
  mission system, testing 52, 53
  player controls code, developing 21
  player, rewarding 197
  tracking systems, adding 49, 50
3D hierarchies 161, 162
_global class 78
_level1 class 78

A

AddScore condition
  creating 191
**Application.LoadLevelAdditive() method
    202**

B

base scripts
  about 28
  CustomGameObj helper class 28
  ObjectInteraction helper class 28

C

camera code
  developing 15
  GameCam.cs, implementing 16
CameraLookPlayer() 207
camera system 11

ChangeState() method 88, 203
character representation
  building 14, 15
character system
  about 11
  developing 13
clickable text elements
  creating 102
  leaving mouse over, detecting 102
  mouse clicks, detecting 102
  mouse over, detecting 102
code changes
  reflecting 89
code functionality
  analysis 90
condition_closerThanThresh script
  about 127
  implementing 132
condition_fartherThanThresh script
  about 128
  implementing 133
controls system 11
core classes, Finding the facts game
  FlagLocators, creating 61
  FlagMonument, creating 61
  flag Prefabs, creating 67-69
  FoundAllTheFlags Prefab, creating 72, 73
  InventoryPlaceOnMonument class,
    creating 63
  mission manager, configuring 74
  MissionMgrHelper script, creating 63
  mission pop-up Prefab, creating 71, 72
  mission reward Prefabs, creating 72
  MonumentMgr, creating 61, 62
  pop-up card Prefabs, creating 70

ReturnedTheFlagsResult Prefab, creating 73, 74

SetupMissionOne script, creating 65, 66

terrain, creating 58-60

TriviaCardScript script, creating 64

CorrectResponse GameObject 182

CorrectResponse Prefabs

creating 187

CustomGameObj class 28

CustomGameObj script

implementing 30, 31

D

DecisionMgr class

testing 135, 136

DisplayInventory method

implementing 40-43

E

e-learning 8

e-learning game

character system, developing 13

distributing 219, 220

features 10

first scene, building 12

GameCam script, extending 142, 143

gamification 8

Geography Quest 10

mission, adding to missionMgr script 142

mission two framework, defining 140, 141

mission two structure, exploring 140

playing 219, 220

reviewing 220

terrain, modifying 143

e-learning game framework

additive load, using 202, 203

delete/load patterns, using 203, 204

level 2, refactoring 210

level 3, refactoring 216-219

pop-up system, refactoring 204

SetupMission2 script, updating 214, 215

system, implementing for connecting object references 211-214

work, refactoring 204

F

Finding the facts game

about 55

components 55

core classes, implementing 58

designing 57

playing 75

teaching loop 58

Finding the facts game components

FlagLocators 55

MissionMgrHelper 56

Monument 56

MonumentMgr 56

SetupMissionOne 56

SimpleDetachScript 56

terrain 56

TriviaCardScript 56

finish line flag

creating 145, 146

Finite State Machine (FSM)

about 84

classes, implementing 86

implementing, in game 85

Switch Case FSM 85, 86

FlagLocators

creating 61

FlagMonument

creating 61

flag Prefabs

creating 67-69

FoundAllTheFlags Prefab

creating 72, 73

G

GameCam.cs

implementing 16-20

GameCam script

extending 142, 143

GameMgr script

about 78

implementing 86-88

GameObjects

about 78, 182

CorrectResponse 182

LevelLogicObj 182
MissionMgr 182
Player 182
QuizCard 182
reorganizing, in Scene view 78
SetupLevel3 182
Time 182
gamification, e-learning
active learning 9
cognitive flow 9
emotional attachment 9
immersion 8
reinforcement and conditioning 9
safe practice environment 10
spatial learning 9
global scene
creating 79, 80
GUI.Button class
clickable button, creating 103
mouse click, detecting 104
UnityGUI, using 103
GUIButton component 98
GUIButton object
exploring 103
GUIText component
about 98
exploring 99
members, interpreting 99
GUITexture component
exploring 98-100

I

in-place animation
versus, root motion animation 170
InteractiveObj class
about 28
OnCollisionEnter() method 32
OnTriggerEnter() method 32
Start() method 32
Update() method 32
interactive object
about 28
building 29
CustomGameObj script, implementing
30, 31

DisplayInventory method, implementing
40-42
InteractiveObj script, implementing 31, 32
InventoryItem script, implementing 34, 35
InventoryMgr script, implementing 36-39
MissionMgr script, implementing 44, 45
Mission script, implementing 46-48
MissionToken script, implementing 48
ObjectInteraction script, implementing
33, 34
SimpleLifespanScript, implementing 48, 49
InteractiveObj script
creating 31
implementing 31-33
InventoryItem class 34
InventoryItem script
implementing 34, 35
InventoryMgr class
about 28, 36
Add() method 37
DisplayInventory method 40
Insert() method 39
Start() method 36
InventoryMgr script
implementing 36-39
InventoryPlaceOnMonument class
creating 63
Inverse Kinematics (IK) 165

L

LERP (linear interpolation) 18
LEVEL1 scene
creating 80, 81
Level2Extras script 211
level2Init script 212
LevelFinished pop up
creating 147, 148
LevelLogicObj GameObject
about 182
implementing 152-158
LevelLogicObj object
modifying 196, 197
LevelStart pop up
creating 147, 148

M

MainCamera GameObject 205
main menu pop up
  building 104-112
Mechanim animation system
  about 165
  appropriate animations, selecting 166
  character script, adding 171, 172
  in-place animation, versus root motion
    animation 170
  quizracer animation FSM, building 174-176
  simple character animation FSM, building
    166-170
  zombie racer animation FSM, building
    172, 173
Mission class 29, 46
MissionMgr class
  about 28, 29, 44
  Add(missionToken) method 44
  ValidateAll() method 46
  Validate(mission) method 45
missionMgr GameObject 182
MissionMgrHelper script
  creating 63
MissionMgr script
  implementing 44, 45
mission pop-up Prefab
  creating 71, 72
mission reward Prefabs
  creating 72
mission system
  testing 52, 53
mission three
  data condition, adding 189
  GameObjects 182
  learning theory, applying 183
  setupLevel3 Prefab, using 189, 190
  structure, creating 184
  terrain, modifying 184
  visitors, adding to park 185
MissionToken class 29, 48
mission two, eLearning game
  adding, to missionMgr script 142
  finish line flag, creating 145, 146
  framework, defining 140, 141
  GameCam script, extending 142, 143

LevelFinished pop up, creating 147, 148
LevelLogicObj GameObject, implementing
    152-158
LevelStart pop up, creating 147, 148
NpcRacers, adding 143, 144
raceStartup Prefab, creating 150, 151
setupLevel2 Prefab, creating 149, 150
start line flag, creating 145, 146
structure, exploring 140
terrain, modifying 143
MonumentMgr
  creating 61

N

NPC conditions
  condition_closerThanThresh script,
    implementing 132
  condition_fartherThanThresh script,
    implementing 133, 134
  response_changeState script, implementing
    134, 135
npcCondition script
  implementing 128
npcDecisionMgr script
  implementing 131
NPC decision system
  implementing 127
  npcCondition, implementing 127, 128
  npcDecisionMgr, implementing
    127, 131, 132
  npcInteraction, implementing 127-130
  npcResponse, implementing 127, 129
  working 127
NPC GameObject
  creating 116
npcInteraction script
  implementing 129, 130
NpcLocators Prefab
  creating 186
NpcRacers
  adding, to mission 143, 144
npcResponse script
  implementing 129
npcScript class
  implementing 116-118

O

ObjectInteraction class
about 28
HandleInteraction() method 34
ObjectInteraction script
implementing 33, 34

P

player controls code
developing 21
PlayerControls.cs, implementing 21-25
PlayerData script 78
Player GameObject 182
player motion algorithm
updating 94
pop-up card Prefabs
creating 70
PopupMainMenu GameObject
creating 82-84
PopupMgr script 213
pop-up system
developing 98
modifying 185, 186
testing 113
pop-up system, refactoring
level 1 pop ups, updating 208, 209
level 2 pop ups, updating 207
level 3 pop ups, updating 205, 206

Q

QuizCard GameObject 182
quiz cards
modifying 187, 188
quizracer animation FSM
building 174, 175

R

raceStartup Prefab
creating 150, 151
refactoring 78
response_changeState script 128
implementing 134
ReturnedTheFlagsResult Prefab
creating 73, 74

S

scenes
adding, to game project 81, 82
ScorePlate
making active 92, 93
setupLevel2 Prefab
creating 149, 150
SetupLevel3 GameObject 182
setupLevel3 Prefab
using 189
SetupMission2 script
updating 214, 215
SetupMission() method 215
SetupMissionOne script
creating 65
SetupMissionThree() script 218
ShowLevel3Results response
creating 192, 193
simple character animation FSM
building 166-170
SimpleLifespanScript class 28, 48
skinned mesh
about 162
character model, acquiring 162-164
character model, importing 163, 164
SplineMgr class
connecting, to NPCScript 124-126
implementing 119-123
start line flag
creating 145, 146
Switch Case FSM 85
systems
updating 91

T

teaching loop, Finding the facts game
application stage 58
presentation stage 58
synthesis stage 58
terrain
creating 58, 60
TextMesh component
about 98
exploring 101
using 102

Time GameObject 182
Time object
 creating 193-195
TriviaCardScript script
 creating 64

U

Unity3D
 skinned mesh 162
Unity animation editor
 about 177
 exploring 177-179
UnityGUI
 using 103
UnityScript object
 exploring 103

Unity UI systems
 GUIButton 98
 GUIText 98
 GUITexture 98
 TextMesh 98
Update() loop 17, 88
UpdateMovement() method 22
UpdateRotAndTrans() custom method 17
UpdateRotAndTrans() method 17, 18

V

Validate() method 92

Z

zombie racer animation FSM
 building 172, 173

Thank you for buying
Creating E-Learning Games with Unity

About Packt Publishing

Packt, pronounced 'packed', published its first book "*Mastering phpMyAdmin for Effective MySQL Management*" in April 2004 and subsequently continued to specialize in publishing highly focused books on specific technologies and solutions.

Our books and publications share the experiences of your fellow IT professionals in adapting and customizing today's systems, applications, and frameworks. Our solution based books give you the knowledge and power to customize the software and technologies you're using to get the job done. Packt books are more specific and less general than the IT books you have seen in the past. Our unique business model allows us to bring you more focused information, giving you more of what you need to know, and less of what you don't.

Packt is a modern, yet unique publishing company, which focuses on producing quality, cutting-edge books for communities of developers, administrators, and newbies alike. For more information, please visit our website: www.packtpub.com.

About Packt Open Source

In 2010, Packt launched two new brands, Packt Open Source and Packt Enterprise, in order to continue its focus on specialization. This book is part of the Packt Open Source brand, home to books published on software built around Open Source licences, and offering information to anybody from advanced developers to budding web designers. The Open Source brand also runs Packt's Open Source Royalty Scheme, by which Packt gives a royalty to each Open Source project about whose software a book is sold.

Writing for Packt

We welcome all inquiries from people who are interested in authoring. Book proposals should be sent to author@packtpub.com. If your book idea is still at an early stage and you would like to discuss it first before writing a formal book proposal, contact us; one of our commissioning editors will get in touch with you.

We're not just looking for published authors; if you have strong technical skills but no writing experience, our experienced editors can help you develop a writing career, or simply get some additional reward for your expertise.

Unity Android Game Development by Example Beginner's Guide

ISBN: 978-1-84969-201-4   Paperback: 320 pages

Learn how to create exciting games using Unity 3D for Android with the help of hands-on examples

1. Enter the increasingly popular mobile market and create games using Unity 3D and Android.

2. Learn optimization techniques for efficient mobile games.

3. Clear, step-by-step instructions for creating a complete mobile game experience.

Unity Multiplayer Games

ISBN: 978-1-84969-232-8   Paperback: 242 pages

Build engaging, fully functional, multiplayer games with Unity engine

1. Create a variety of multiplayer games and apps in the Unity 4 game engine, still maintaining compatibility with Unity 3.

2. Employ the most popular networking middleware options for Unity games.

3. Packed with ideas, inspiration, and advice for your own game design and development.

Please check **www.PacktPub.com** for information on our titles

Unity 4.x Game Development by Example Beginner's Guide

ISBN: 978-1-84969-526-8   Paperback: 572 pages

A seat-of-your-pants manual for building fun, groovy little games quickly with Unity 4.x

1. Learn the basics of the Unity 3D game engine by building five small, functional game projects.

2. Explore simplification and iteration techniques that will make you more successful as a game developer.

3. Take Unity for a spin with a refreshingly humorous approach to technical manuals.

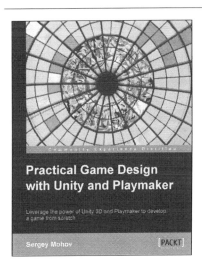

Practical Game Design with Unity and Playmaker

ISBN: 978-1-84969-810-8   Paperback: 122 pages

Leverage the power of Unity 3D and Playmaker to develop a game from scratch

1. Create artificial intelligence for a game using Playmaker.

2. Learn how to integrate a game with external APIs (Kongregate).

3. Learn how to quickly develop games in Unity and Playmaker.

4. A step-by-step game development tutorial using AI scripting, external APIs, and Multiplayer implementation.

Please check **www.PacktPub.com** for information on our titles

Made in the USA
Lexington, KY
04 October 2014